A Concise Handbook of Business Research
Special Emphasis on Data Analysis Using MS-Excel and R

A Concise Handbook of Business Research

Special Emphasis on Data Analysis Using MS-Excel and R

Authors

Ashish Arya
Vishnu Nath
Pankaj Madan

LONDON AND NEW YORK

First published 2024
by Routledge
4 Park Square, Milton Park, Abingdon, Oxon OX14 4RN

and by Routledge
605 Third Avenue, New York, NY 10158

Routledge is an imprint of the Taylor & Francis Group, an informa business

© 2024 Manakin Press

The right of Ashish Arya, Vishnu Nath and Pankaj Madan to be identified as author of this work has been asserted in accordance with sections 77 and 78 of the Copyright, Designs and Patents Act 1988.

All rights reserved. No part of this book may be reprinted or reproduced or utilised in any form or by any electronic, mechanical, or other means, now known or hereafter invented, including photocopying and recording, or in any information storage or retrieval system, without permission in writing from the publishers.

Trademark notice: Product or corporate names may be trademarks or registered trademarks, and are used only for identification and explanation without intent to infringe.

Print edition not for sale in South Asia (India, Sri Lanka, Nepal, Bangladesh, Pakistan or Bhutan)

British Library Cataloguing-in-Publication Data
A catalogue record for this book is available from the British Library

ISBN: 9781032567525 (hbk)
ISBN: 9781032567532 (pbk)
ISBN: 9781003436980 (ebk)

DOI: 10.4324/9781003436980

Typeset in Times New Roman
by Manakin Press, Delhi

Contents

Abbreviations

Chapter 1: Introduction to Business Research, Research Process,   **1–30**
Secondary Data Research, and Its Tools and Techniques.

1.1	Definition, Nature, and Scope of Business Research	2
1.2	Role of Business Research in Decision Making	3
1.3	Nature of Business Research	4
1.4	Applications of Business Research	5
1.5	Management Decision Problem vs Business Research Problem	6
1.6	The Research Process	6
1.7	The Research Proposal	9
1.8	The format for Dissertation/Project Work	10
1.9	Ethical Issues in Your Research Work	12
1.10	Research Problem and Its Formulation	13
	1.10.1 Writing a Problem and the Purpose Statement in Your Project/Thesis.	15
	1.10.2 From Where to Search for a Good Problem to Work on?	16
1.11	Literature Review	17
1.12	Research Design	19
1.13	Types of Research	21
	1.13.1 Exploratory Research (A Type of Qualitative Research)	22
	1.13.2 Descriptive Research (A Type of Quantitative Study)	22
	1.13.3 Casual and Correlational (A Type of Quantitative Study)	23
1.14	Validity in Experiment: Internal and External Validity	24

A Concise Handbook of Business Research

1.15 Secondary Data Research	25
1.15.1 Secondary Data advantages and Disadvantages	25
1.15.2 Criteria for Evaluating Secondary Sources	26
1.15.3 Secondary Data Sources in the Indian Context	26
1.16 Syndicate Research:	28
Tentative Exam Questions	28

Chapter 2: Primary Data Research and Its Tools and Techniques 31–38

2.1 Primary Data	31
2.1.1 Collecting Primary Data: Survey, Observation, and Interview	32
2.1.2 Survey Methods: Questionnaire and Interview Method	32
2.1.3 Observation Method	33
2.2 Random Sample Collection Method	34
2.3 Survey vs Observations	35
2.4 Comparison of Self-Administered, Telephone, Mail, e-mails Techniques	35
2.5 Which Method to Use in a Study	36
Tentative Exam Questions	37

Chapter 3: Measurement, Scaling and Sampling   **39–56**

3.1 Concept of Measurement	39
3.2 Concept of Scaling	40
3.3 Scales of Measurement	40
3.4 Scaling Techniques for Measurement	42
3.5 Questionnaire-Form & Design	44
3.5.1 Mode of Presenting a Questionnaire	45
3.5.2 Important Points on Questionnaire Design	45
3.6 Fundamentals of Scale Evaluation	47
3.6.1 Reliability	47
3.6.2 Validity	48
3.6.3 Generalizability	49

Contents

3.7 Sampling	49
3.7.1 Sample	50
3.7.2 Sampling Techniques	50
3.7.3 Determination of Sample Size	53
3.8 Cronbach Alpha Test for Reliability (Using Software)	55
Tentative Exam Questions	55
Chapter 4: Data and Method of Analysis (Using Excel and R)	**57–120**
4.1 Introduction to Excel and R for Statistical Data Analysis	57
4.2 Introduction to R	58
4.3 Data and Method of Analysis	66
4.3.1 Data Visualization	68
4.3.2 Bivariate Analysis	78
4.3.3 Multivariate Analysis	115
Tentative Exam Questions	118
Chapter 5: Improving Academic Writing (Additional Chapter)	**121–128**
5.1 Referencing and In-text Citation	121
5.1.1 Adding In-text Citation and References in MS -Word 2016	122
5.2 Plagiarism, What it is? How to Detect? and How-to Remove?	125
5.2.1 Plagiarism Detection and Removal	126
5.3 Improve Your Academic Writing Using Free Software Grammarly	127
Tentative Exam Questions	128
References	**129–132**
1.1 Random Number Table	133–139
2.1 Standardized Normal Distribution	140–141
3.1 Critical Value of t	142–142
4.1 Critical Value of Chi-Square (x^2)	143–143
5.1 Critical Value of F	144–148
Index	**149-152**

Abbreviations

ANOVA	Analysis of Variance
AICTE	All India Council for Technical Education
APA	American Psychological Association
BBA	Bachelor of Business Administration
CBCS	Choice Based Credit System
CA	Charted Accountant
CRAN	Comprehensive R Archive Network
EFA	Exploratory Factor Analysis
E.g./e.g.	Example
Etc./etc.	Etcetera
FMS	Faculty of Management Studies
GBR	Gurukul Business Review
GST	Goods and Service Tax
GUI	Graphics User Interface
IDE	Integrated Development Environment
IIT	Indian Institute of Technology
ITL	Income Tax Lawyer
MANOVA	Multivariate Analysis of Variance
MBA	Master of Business Administration
PCA	Principal Component Analysis
Ph.D.	Doctor of Philosophy
RM	Research Methodology
SRL	Syndicate Research Limited
SPSS	Earlier known as Statistical Package for Social Sciences but now is Known as IBM SPSS
UGC	University Grant Commission

1

Introduction to Business Research, Research Process, Secondary Data Research, and Its Tools and Techniques

Syllabus Unit 1: *Nature and Scope of Business Research – Role of Business Research in decision making, Nature of business research, Applications of Business Research; The Research process – Steps in the research process; the research proposal; Ethical issues, Problem Formulation: Management decision problem vs. Business Research problem. Research Design: Exploratory, Descriptive & Causal. Validity in experimentation-internal validity and external validity. Secondary Data Research: Advantages & Disadvantages of Secondary Data, Criteria for evaluating secondary sources, secondary sources of data in the Indian Context, Syndicated Research (in India)*

*"To discuss that the way we thought it is,
isn't the way it is, is not failure it's knowledge"*

—**Michael Quinn Patton**

(1)

2 A Concise Handbook of Business Research

1.1 Definition, Nature, and Scope of Business Research

Explaining the term business research requires an understanding of the three terms 'Business', 'Business Organization' and 'Research'.

Business means any commercial activity in which there is a seller and a buyer and the seller sells the thing in exchange for money. Any organization performing this activity by selling either goods or services or something in this continuum can be called as a *Business Organization*. The prime objective of any business organization is to *maximize its profit* which requires lots of decision making by the company people, especially the managers.

The word *Research* i*n* a very simple sense can be defined as a systematic investigation into an underlying problem before reaching a final conclusion. It helps a business organization and its managers in their decision making by studying a problem in a systematic manner, providing solutions that are supported by evidences, using scientific tools and techniques, and is well documented e.g. your project/dissertation report. Let us look at some good definitions to get to the core of the word 'Research':

Creswell (2017) defines the term 'research' as a " *process of steps used to collect and analyze information to increase understanding of the topic or an issue*".

> *What is this **-Creswell(2017)** above ?*
>
> *It is 'citation'. When ever we refer to someone's published work (here the defination of research by john W. Creswell) in our project/thesis/book, we give credit to the author of that writeup, as it is his work and not ours. We also use citation and referencing to convert our weak argument into a strong argument by providing support of evidences to our statements. To learn more on it and how to do citation and referencing in MS- word, see chapter five in detail.*

This definition says that there is a topic or an issue which requires further development of knowledge, and for that we need to collect some data. The collected data further needs some analysis to reach the desired objective.

According to Wilson (2014), a work to be considered as a research work should satisfy three following characteristics:

1. There should be an inquiry or investigation into a problem.
2. A step by step methodology should be followed.
3. The knowledge about the problem and the subject of interest should be increased.

If these three conditions remain unsatisfied the word 'Research' is not justified. Understanding the basics of business and research, we are in a position to explain the term 'Business Research'. Let us start with a standard definition given by Cooper & Schindler (2014). According to him, *"**Business Research** is a systematic inquiry that provides information to guide managerial decisions. More specifically, it is a process of planning, acquiring, analyzing, and disseminating relevant data, information, and insights to decision makers in ways that mobilize the organization to take appropriate actions that, in turn, maximize performance and reduces risks."*

So, we can say that in order to maximize business performance and to reduce associated risk, research helps managers in decision making by providing solutions obtained in a systematic manner, and supported by strong evidences.

Do not worry if you still have some doubts, read the chapter till the end and then ask the question to self, *"Did I understood the term business research?"* If still the answer is no, talk to your class teacher.

1.2 Role of Business Research in Decision Making

When we talk about business we talk about investment and return. Every business organization works for profit, and to maximize its profit it has to either decrease its cost, increase its price, or increase its 'sales'

4 A Concise Handbook of Business Research

(Apart from understanding its customers). But in the complex and dynamic business environment, it is not an easy task considering the hurdles produced by the environment, e.g. increasing price of a product when it does not differ much from other products may lead to switching of customers. Research helps in decision making by providing solutions to a problem, which are thoroughly investigated, both theoretically and scientifically, *e.g. an outcome of a research work may show that it is better to launch a new product in region 'x' then in region 'y' because there are fewer customers in region 'y', and their taste and preferences does not match the product to be launched.*

Today's research environment is supported by high technology tools like R and MS Excel, having the power to provide some deep insights into the data.

1.3 Nature of Business Research

The nature of business research can be summarized as:

- *It is a systematic study:* Means the study will consist of certain steps to be followed before reaching a final conclusion.

- *Informs managerial decision making:* It helps managers to evaluate the alternatives on the basis of some strong justification produced by research.

- *Requires extraction of information from raw data:* The world is full of raw data e.g. a number of malnutrition children in a village in Haridwar district of Uttarakhand, and the number of food supplements available in the market for children below 05 years. We need to get to the source and to the information required for our study.

- *Requires variables and their measurement:* The problem to be solved needs to be converted into variables such that it can be measured. If you cannot quantity your problem you cannot measure it.

Introduction to Business Research, Research Process 5

- *Requires validation:* The methodology we use, the findings we generate out of research requires validation. Validation means providing justification to the facts and findings we produced. It is about answering the questions, whether the output produced make sense or not? why was the particular methodology used? Whether the methodology used is measuring what it was supposed to?

- *Systematic presentation:* The outcome of research has to be properly documented in a systematic manner e.g. Your project report, dissertation report, thesis or executive company report.

1.4 Applications of Business Research

Research has its applications in almost all the functions of business, whether it is finance, marketing, human resource or supply chain. Let us elaborate a few:

1. For *finance personnel,* analyzing the initial impact of goods and service tax (GST) on trade and commerce or measuring the liquidity of firms in two different industries will require the application of research.

2. For *human resource personnel,* problems related to recruitment and selection, performance appraisal, employee behavior, attitude, leadership can be well scrutinized with the help of research.

3. For *production personnel,* the objective could be of minimizing wastes on the basis of some benchmarking practices, research will play an important role in dealing with these issues.

4. For *marketing personnel,* objectives of studying brand loyalty, product positioning, market segmentation, increasing the product market penetration can be analyzed with the help of research.

These are just a few examples to showcases the potential of research in improving the decision-making structure of the company's different departments. As mentioned, the constantly changing environment poses a threat to the company survival & growth, and to overcome this the

6 A Concise Handbook of Business Research

organizations continuously study the environment. But those working with the help of research are certainly going to have an edge.

1.5 Management Decision Problem vs. Business Research Problem

One of the important roles of business research is to generate information that helps a decision maker in making an optimum decision (Bajpai, 2011). The business problem of simple nature which can be solved with the help of repetitive measures do not need the help of research too often. However, the problem of complex nature, *e.g. What should be the best time to launch a new product? What should be the initial price for the new product in a low-profit-margin segment?* May require the help of systematic research work. This book is a complete package to help the management graduates in understanding the methodology required to convert the management problems into a business research problem.

1.6 The Research Process

The research process is a series of steps to be followed while conducting research. Going through various books on research methodology and our own personal experience, the following steps are essential in any research work.

- *Establish an intention* (Wilson, 2014).
- *Choose a research topic and formulate a research problem* (Kothari, 2004; Wilson, 2014).
- *Conduct a preliminary or simple literature review* (Machi & McEvoy, 2016) *and find reasons to continue your research further.*
- *Conduct a rigorous or complex literature review* (Machi & McEvoy, 2016) *to get close to the problem.*
- *Set hypotheses and then go for proving it* (We use it in quantitative studies more, where you work using statistical tools like mean, standard deviation, t-test, ANOVA, correlation and regression analysis).

Introduction to Business Research, Research Process **7**

- *Define the research design or strategies of inquiry* (Denzin, 2011; Creswell, Research Design:4th ed., 2014). It is something like making a well-documented plan to win a football match, by producing everything on the paper.
- *Take the necessary permissions.*
- *Collect data as per the set strategies of inquiry* (Wilson, 2014; Kothari, 2004).
- *Analyze data and test the set hypotheses* (Wilson, 2014; Kothari, 2004).
- *Sharing the results* (Zikmund, Babin, & Carr, 2009) *through reports, thesis or research papers in a journal.*

Detailed explanation: Every research work starts with an *intention*. The intention for you studying this Research Methodology subject is that it a part of your course curriculum, and if you do not read it and pass it, you will not be promoted to the next class. Similarly, when we enter the field of research work there is a background intention. Like those who want to enter in the field of teaching needs to complete their Ph.D. which is rigorous research work. *The intentions set the boundaries for work with respect to the time frame, the cost involved and the deep insight needed.* Like for the BBA project you got two to three months whereas for Ph.D. you got two to five years.

The second and prime element of the research process is choosing a research topic and formulating the research problem. *Your topic is the broad theme you work on,* e.g. performance appraisal in human resource management, the supply chain for production peoples etc. *Under your research topic area, you choose a research problem.* The problem is something you are going to work on for your entire project. Formulating it such that it can be researched is key to quality research work.

The third step is about conducting a preliminary literature review and finding reasons to continue your research further. *Doing a simple literature review from business reports, business articles, few selected research papers sets the theme and let you know should you move further with the current problem or not?* If you find that lots of solutions are

8 A Concise Handbook of Business Research

there already or your problem then either you can combine and present the results of those studies (*more of a meta-analysis approach*) or you can drop that problem and look for something novel and useful in current and future context. Doing a preliminary literature review you can get these two outcomes (though they may extend to complex literature review):

1. You found a model to study your problem and then you move further with your study (more a type of quantitative study, discussed in the research design section later).

2. You did not find a model for your problem and you try to explore variables and model to study the problem (more a type of qualitative study, discussed in the research design section later).

Then post-finalization of your topic, problem and your title, you conduct a rigorous literature review to get close to the problem and derive its solution (*complex literature review*). At the end of complex literature review work you come up with a conceptual map for your study, types of variables, their relationship and the literature gap in the context of your problem (You might say, *"this is it what I was looking for, and this is I am able to extract from the past studies on this problem"*).

Post literature review, after we have seen the relationship among variables we then set hypotheses *i.e. we go with some set assumptions about the relationship among variables*, e.g. there is no relationship between reading my book on RM and you getting good marks in it. *Setting up a hypothesis provides the direction for your study.*

After all the hard work done till this stage, here comes the most important stage of the research process, '*Research Design*'. *Research design or strategies of inquiry* (Denzin, 2011) *is the combination of methods, procedures, and style used by the researcher to meet his desired objective(s).* It is the best possible structure to study the formulated problem, questions under investigation and finally, the topic decided. It is the blueprint of the psychological view of your study, the approach you are going to take to conduct your research, and the methods you will use to support the approach undertaken. Broadly the essence of the topic under study, the researcher's worldview of his surroundings and

Introduction to Business Research, Research Process **9**

the expertise of the researcher with quantitative or qualitative research methods will decide the type of research design a researcher chooses.

The next step after the research design is to take the necessary permission before you move on to data collection. *Like at times, organizations do not entertain anyone for a survey without prior approval taken in writing.*

Now as you got the necessary permissions, go for data collection. Data collection can again take place in two parts. *One is pilot or sample data collection,* which is performed to check the reliability, validity, necessary changes to be made in the instrument or to check the shape and size of the output. After performing the necessary changes in the instrument go for *rigorous data collection.* The moment you collect the data as desired, you put the set hypothesis under statistical lenses using data analysis tools and techniques and see what your findings are. *The moment you are done with all research work now, it is the time to share the results with your academic and industry community.* The publication is in the form of project reports for BBA students, dissertation reports for MBA students, thesis for Ph.D. students, and research papers who wants to publish their work in a journal.

1.7 The Research Proposal

Your project completion deals with two important documents: one is a synopsis or your research proposal, and other is the complete document of your research work submitted at the end of the semester/year when you are done with your project.

The *synopsis* is a short write up of your research work which you are proposing to study. It contains your title, the research questions (which you want to answer with the help of your study), objective(s) of the study, tentative research methodology and significance of your research work. *The synopsis is the trailer of the big picture you might be trying to show out of your research work.* It is subjected to frequent revisions by the reviewing committee or by your supervisor. The simple reason being, your supervisor may have low confidence in the topic or the outcome of the research work it is going to produce, e.g. the topic of your proposed

10 A Concise Handbook of Business Research

study may look too long and abstract to be completed on time, so the reviewing committee may ask you for revision and bring the modified synopsis in the next meeting.

The *Dissertation/Project report* is the big picture of your synopsis. This is a document which you finally present for defending your degree or semester or a subject as per your university curriculum. *The Dissertation has a more formal structure than synopsis which generally varies from university to university*, e.g. the front page of a Dissertation report might be different for two universities; the referencing style (citation of other researchers work) use to sight others work might be APA (American Psychological Association) style for one university, and might be Harvard style for another, so do check with the institution or with your supervisor for the contents and style for your report.

Some key points and a tentative format for your synopsis.

- It is of (2-15 pages)
- It contains a title page
- It contains a section, 'Introduction to the study'.
- It contains your 'Purpose Statement' which also includes your research questions. Your purpose statement can be written as a separate aim and objectives statement also.
- The synopsis requires a tentative 'Research Methodology', that is, what methods you will use, what style of inquiry you will use and what philosophical assumption is holding behind your problem-solving thinking. In short, the total set of activities you will be taking to solve your problem.
- The section on the 'Significance of Your Research Work', that is, who is going to benefits from your work output.

For more details on synopsis you should contact your subject teacher or project incharge.

1.8 The Format for Dissertation/Project Work

Dissertation format is the more extended version of your research proposal and it includes all the steps we talked about in the research process.

Some supervisors like the traditional style of presenting the research work, whereas, some like the modern trend. In the tradition trend, things move the same way as your research process and they become chapters, whereas in modern trend different headings are there which resembles your different objectives. Though the majority of the part remains same, there is a pinch of change in the format from researcher to researcher, from university to university, or supervisor to supervisor. Our suggestion is to check with your institution guidelines for making the dissertation file/thesis. Let us see review some format. The first format discussed is inspired by (Creswell, Research Design:4th ed., 2014).

Format 1:

Introduction

- Statement of the problem
- Purpose of the study
- Research Questions or hypothesis
- Theoretical perspective

Review of Literature

Methods

- Type of research design (e.g. Experimental, survey)
- Population, sample, and participants
- Data collection instruments, variables, and materials
- Data analysis procedures
- Anticipated ethical or pilot Test
- Preliminary studies or pilot tests
- Appendix: Instruments, timelines, and proposed budget

If format looks new and bit complicated to you then you can follow a simple yet effective format as stated, it is followed by most Indian colleges and universities and still a classical format:

Format 2:

- Bonafide Certificate
- Abstract

12 A Concise Handbook of Business Research

- Acknowledgment
- List of tables and figures
- List of abbreviations and acronyms used
- Introduction
- The objective(s) of the study
- Review of literature
- Research methodology
- Data analysis and interpretation
- Results and discussion
- Conclusion and suggestions
- Limitations
- References
- Appendix

1.9 Ethical Issues in Your Research Work

Ethics is about conducting your research work without involving in any matter which can come under unfair means. It is about pursuing your work with discipline, without copying others work, and if using others work it needs to be cited properly. Some of the important points which can raise ethical issues in your research work are highlighted below:

- **Stick to the important dates in concern to your proposal:** Failing to do so can lead to many flawed activities e.g. Starting late on your project report will make you nervous and ultimately it will lead to a shabby work or a copy paste of other's work. Copying in the publication world (like books, thesis, project reports) is called 'plagiarism' which is not allowed at all. Your supervisor surely will catch you and it will lead to consequences like failing in your project work. So, make sure you start on time and your work is plagiarism free.
- **Maintain privacy of the participants if they want:** Here participants mean the respondents from whom you filled out

your questionnaire or interviewed. Without their consent do not publish their details.

- **Take necessary permission concerning your study:** Taking necessary permission helps you to get genuine data and helps in data collection.

- **Do not fill fake data in your study:** At any point of time if the amount of data you want to collect for your research work remains insufficient, do not ever fill fake data, as it may further lead to negative consequences. E.g. if a researcher is measuring the impact of Desprin on headache and If he is not able to collect the data on time, think about what will happen if he produces his report using fake data? His study may show that Desprin does not have an impact on headache, whereas it actually has. The result, some people may stop buying desprin which is not correct at all.

- **Do not manipulate data:** Do not manipulate data for the type of answers you want your study to show as an outcome. Let the data outcome flow naturally from your study. Always be at the center of the problem and do not be biased to any conclusion until and unless you prove it. As said by Michael Quinn Patton *"Finding that the world is, isn't the way it, is not a failure, it's knowledge"*. The world is the way it is, you cannot change it. Present the work as it comes out. In the hard times, when your research output is not showing any significant output, do not feel low, look for the probable reasons (*why the output is not significant?*) and use your writing skills to highlight them. Research is not only about finding hidden truths, but it is also about presenting your work such that people love to read it.

Now let us start with a detail discussion on the important steps in the research process.

1.10 Research Problem and Its Formulation

Research problems are the subject area issues, controversies or concerns that guide the need for conducting a particular study. *It is a topic which*

14 A Concise Handbook of Business Research

has caught your eyes, which you think is interesting, which you think is still unsolved, and which you think you should work on for your project, dissertation or thesis.

While taking a problem at hand make sure of the following two points/questions:

- *The problem should be relevant, important and should have some future* (Hamming, 2016). Study the problem which can add to the pool of knowledge.
- You should ask two questions to yourself. *Can it be researched? and, are the resources and skills available to solve the problem?*

Formulation of a problem means, to provide a structure to the problem such that it can be studied and can be measured. One strategy in formulating a problem is to write a well-defined problem statement which is a clear, precise, and short statement of the question or issue that is to be investigated with the goal of finding an answer or solution (Sekaran, 2003).

(Wilson, 2014) mentioned three key elements to get closer to the problem under investigation:

1. Clearly defined set of research questions.
2. Based on your research questions derive a set of well-defined aim and objective(s) of the study (what we call as purpose statement), and finally,
3. Derive a well-defined title for your study based on the above two points.

However, at times the problem due to its complex nature may require rephrasing many times. For complex problems we are presenting five key steps to get closer to your problem under investigation:

- Define your problems as a set of questions.
- Read literature in the context of your problem.
- Derive a problem statement and purpose statement for your study.
- Derive a well-defined title for your study.
- Rephrase the problem if it of a complex nature (Kothari, 2004).

1.10.1 Writing a Problem and the Purpose Statement in your Project/Thesis.

To discuss these statements, Ph.D. thesis from Indian research database "Shodhganga", website: www.shodhganga.inflibnet.ac.in are taken into consideration.

Here we have used Anand (2016) thesis for discussion. The researcher is from the FPM program from IIM Indore. She elaborated her problem statement in her motivation for the study section (mentioned on page 3 of 6 in chapter 01). The section of which is presented for your reference. See, how she came up with the problem, presented it, and how she supported it with some strong evidence.

The primary motivation for this study came from few observations and then through informal discussions with some friends who are employed in different industries. Thereafter, we went through several reports and literature to look into the statistics and existing researches. According to a recent report (WHO, 2014). India has the highest suicide rate in the world, with almost 2,60,000 suicides in 2012. One of the major attributed behind this is found to be loneliness. A research conducted by Duke University says that the number of Americans between 1985 and 2004, who said there was no one with whom they can discuss their important matters has increased by threefold to 25 percent......

Though loneliness is a predominant workplace emotion (Ozcelik & Barsade, 2011) unfortunately it has received scant attention within the field of management (Erdil & Ertosun, 2011); Ertosin & Erdil, 2012; Lam Lau, 2012; Ozcelik & Barsade, 2011; Wright, 2005; Wright, 2012; Wright, Burt & Strongman, 2006). Given the gap in the literature, in the present study, we attempt to explore the phenomena of loneliness in the workplace.

Source: Anand, P. (2016, March). *Impact and Implications of workplace loneliness: A two sample mixed method study.* **Retrieved from www.shodhganga.inflibnet.ac.in/.**

The purpose of her study is mentioned in her section 'Research Objective' (*see the section of her thesis, page 4 of 6 in chapter 01*). The objectives are presented in term of research questions which her study attempted to satisfy. The section of which is presented for your reference.

16 A Concise Handbook of Business Research

See how beautifully she has written it.

> The present study attempts to explore the factors that impact the experience of loneliness among employees, specifically at their workplace. We believe that understanding the factors that might impact the whole experience of loneliness at work will help the organization to identify how to mitigate the loneliness of their employees within their workplaces. Based on the above discussion, we go ahead with the following research objective in mind-
>
> - To explore whether people experience loneliness at their workplace or not.
> - What factors do affect the experience of workplace loneliness?
>
> The study has been done in Indian context because of three reasons. First, India's workforce, (those between the age group of 15 and 64 years) is expected to rise from almost 64 percent of its population in 2009 to 67 percent in 2020 (DaVanzo et.al.2011). Hence studying loneliness at Indian workplace is of utmost importance. Second, loneliness is a growing phenomenon in the Indian context. For example, lots of helplines have been initiated in India to help out with loneliness and depression. Websites such as your can did friend.com.........etc. have been established to provide shoulders to people who feel lonely or depressed in their personal or professional life..........
>
> **Source: Anand, P. (2016, March).** *Impact and Implications of workplace loneliness: A two sample mixed method study.* **Retrieved from www. shodhganga.inflibnet.ac.in/.**

However, to read further on writing a good purpose statement read Creswell, Research Design:4th ed. (2014).

1.10.2 From Where to Search for a Good Problem to Work on?

Let me elaborate you some good sources to reach your desired objective of finding a good problem to work on:

1. The superstore for looking at a problem is the world around you. *The mass source is the internet.* Go to YouTube, Google and type new business problems thousands of pages will get open, look for interviews of corporate personalities, see seminars of government for businesses.

2. For current problems read business newspapers. We found this exercise very helpful with our students. Further after reading the

Introduction to Business Research, Research Process **17**

article, look for a problem in that article and try to formulate it in a statement. The easiest exercise is to work out on a topic for research from the given article. e.g. *try to build a model of being all India topper in class X and XII exams, from the interview articles of students who had topped in previous exams.*

4. The *old project reports and dissertation reports* in your library are very good sources.

5. The Indian databases like '*shodhganga, iitinflibinetkgpndl* can get you thesis and articles.

6. The *contents of your different books*, for e.g. the contents of the books in HRM "Performance Appraisal" or in Marketing "Market Segmentation" will give you starting base to conduct research.

7. Various *open source journal* sites like www.ssrn.com, www.jstor.com or various paid journal sites like www.emeraldinsight.com, if your college or university has a subscription to it.

8. Your *teachers' expertise area* can help you to get a good problem to work on.

This is not an exhaustive list but definitely it will help you further to get to your problem area. Graduate students should start from the subject or book of choice and then should move further on the other sources mentioned.

1.11 Literature Review

Let us understand this topic by answering two questions: **What is a literature review? What is the purpose of conducting the literature review?**

A literature review is a pool of knowledge created by scholars and practitioners around the world by working on a problem and publishing it. This knowledge is present in the *Project Reports (*of your pass out of graduate and postgraduate students); *Ph.D. Thesis* (by doctoral scholars); in J*ournals (*by scholars and practitioners*)*, *Organizations* N*ewsletters, Magazines, Annual Reports* (organization databases) or on the important portals like *www.shrm.org, www.istd.org*. Most of the referred material might be in your institution library. The most trusted are the literature published in the reputed journals and the company databases.

The purpose of conducting a literature review as visible in some of the research work is to review the literature, which is the knowledge created by others. But this is a *passive approach* which sounds as the objective is to collect past literature to fill the section of our references. The recommended is the *active approach* i.e. the purpose of the literature review should be to understand and produce your own *intellectual heritage* or your *intellectual genealogy* (Patton, 2015). This intellectual heritage *(which is your unique work composed of your psychology and methodology used to inquire into your problem area, and the results and findings produced*) is then placed in the pool of knowledge available, to make it updated, e.g. a research work is done on e-governance and its impact on business performance in U.S.A can be used to study the e-governance practices impact on business in India. The outcome of the research work by the Indian candidate will add to the pool of knowledge in the field of e-governance, where the work done of a USA candidate already exist. Let us make it clearer with one more example, *literature review as a pool of knowledge created in the field of Human Resource Management* (fig 1.1 below). Researchers have been

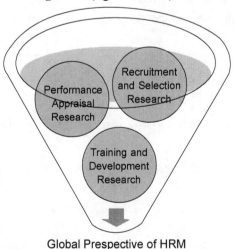

Global Prespective of HRM

Fig. 1.1: Example of Literature Review in the field of HRM

Introduction to Business Research, Research Process **19**

working in all the fields of HRM, like recruitment selection, performance appraisal, training and development, and many more related fields. All the research work produced by the researchers in the mentioned fields is the knowledge, an intellectual heritage of a researcher, which together makes the pool of literature available to study the global perspective of HRM and its functions.

In summary, it can be said that literature review in a research work is not about numbers (as misconceptualized by many researchers), but it is a means of producing quality research work, which is your intellectual heritage, established on the shoulders of other's quality research work. The literature review not only have some direct or indirect solutions to your problem, but they are a bright source of knowledge about the methods of inquiry adopted, approaches, and the thought process of the researchers in a particular setting.

1.12 Research Design

Let us start with the quick review on the research design we mentioned in the research process. Research design or strategies of inquiry (Denzin, 2011) is the combination of *methods, procedures, and style* used by the researcher to meet his desired objective(s). It is the best possible structure to study the formulated problem, questions under investigation and finally, the topic decided. It is the blueprint of the psychological view of your study, the approach you are going to take to conduct your research and the methods you will use to support the approach undertaken. It is basically your research set of activities that will make you solve the research problem undertaken.

Let us describe the research design section in detail by explaining its composition:

1. *Your strategies of inquiry* (Creswell, 2017; Denzin, 2011): Depending upon the nature of the problem and you and your supervisor's expertise, you may choose *quantitative approach* (experimental, correlation or non-experimental survey design)

20 A Concise Handbook of Business Research

or *qualitative approach* (ethnography, grounded theory, narrative research design, case study), or you may choose a combination of these two approaches called as *mixed method research design* (Sequential, concurrent, embedded or transformative). Examples of using these three strategies of inquiry could be:

- If a problem is to be solved using an already defined model, you may choose a quantitative design.

- If a problem is not defined and need to be explored, say for variables, you will go for qualitative design as it not about using scientific tool and techniques like quantitative research. It is about experiencing the living structure, interacting with participants and sensing the environment so that you can understand the problem and/or extract variables for study.

- However at times, there is a problem which is not fully solved with either of the two designs, and for this you need mixed method research designs. Read Creswell, Research Design:4th ed., (2014) for more on research design.

2. *Choosing Research methods* (Creswell,2014; Crotty, 1998): Research methods is a term which deals with the *collection of data* as well as *data analysis*. When we are saying choosing the right research methods, we not only mean selecting the right data collection tools (*interview, observation, survey, focus group discussion*), knowing from whom you going to fill your data from, and what will be your sample size, but we are also referring to right kind of technique to analyze the data (for quantitative study it is about choosing right kind of statistical tool, and in the qualitative study it is about coding the data and converting into small sub-themes, finally to broader themes and then their description).

3. You and your supervisor *epistemological and ontological view* (Crotty, 1998) : Epistemology broadly deals with the question *"How do you know what you know?"* Broadly there are two sets of theories for knowing the world around you. One says that to

Introduction to Business Research, Research Process **21**

study a problem it is best to be separated from the problem and study it, and the second theory says that if you really want to understand the problem you need to experience it by interacting with the participants, e.g. visiting the participant's settings. Whereas the *ontological* view asks the question *"What is the nature of reality?"* That is, to what extent you get close to defining what reality is, *"plants are living creature, so do we humans, and so do animals, the reality is that if you hit anyone, they will feel pain, but sadly some can see only for humans"*. How much you get close to the reality will define how do you study it.

Other than the basic design methodology, let us see some *essentials of research design*:

- Considering the research work as an *activity and time-based plan* (Blumberg, Cooper, & Schindler, 2005).

- The Introduction to your study, the purpose statement, research questions & hypothesis, and the quantitative/qualitative/mixed methods procedures (Creswell, 2014) should support each other and should be well written and explained.

- *Unit of analysis* (Creswell,2014; Rowley, 2002) i.e. who will be the participants or samples in your study should be carefully chosen.

1.13 Types of Research

Depending upon the nature of the problem, research questions, objectives, and hypothesis, your research will broadly fall in either of the two: *Qualitative study or Quantitative study*. Breaking it further the research can be of three types:

1. Exploratory Research

2. Descriptive Research

3. Causal Research

1.13.1 Exploratory Research (A type of Qualitative Research)

In the words of (Sekaran, 2003) exploratory study is undertaken when the problem at hand has not been dealt before (*not much is known about the situation at hand, or no information is available on how similar problems or research issues have been solved in the past*). In such cases, extensive preliminary work needs to be done to gain familiarity with the phenomena in the situation, and understand what is occurring, before we develop a model and set up a rigorous design for a comprehensive investigation. The research procedures look more subjective as the objective is to find the dimensions of the problem. When the data reveal some pattern regarding the phenomena of interest, theories are developed and hypotheses are formulated. e.g. *Leadership theories which keep on upgrading with new dimensions.* In summary, the purpose of exploratory research (Bajpai, 2011) is to:

- Obtaining background information about the problem.
- Formulation of the research problem.
- Identifying and defining the key research variables.
- Developing a Hypothesis.

1.13.2 Descriptive Research (A Type of Quantitative Study)

Descriptive research starts from where the exploratory research end. As mentioned by Zikmund, Babin, & Carr (2009) the major purpose of this type of research is to *describe the characteristics of key variables in your research* e.g. The characteristics of objects, people, groups, organizations, or environments relevant to your study. It defines your key variables by addressing *who, what, when, where, and how questions.* e.g. the unemployment and employment data of different states available on the government portals of different countries. (check https://data.gov.in/). It is *structured and systematic in comparison to exploratory research.* Examples of a descriptive study output can be a study on a BBA class student in terms of sex composition, age groupings, and the number of certificate courses taken.

Quite frequently, *descriptive studies are undertaken in organizations to learn about and describe the characteristics of a group of employees*, as for example, the age, educational level, job status and, length of service in the system. Descriptive studies are also *undertaken to understand the characteristics of organizations that follow certain common practices*. For example, one might want to know the characteristics of banking companies. Your survey designs become part of it.

1.13.3 Casual and Correlational (A Type of Quantitative study)

At times the problem is of nature where one variable (e.g. Advertisement) is affecting the other (e.g. Sales of the organization). In this type of studies, the researcher is interested in finding the *relationship and the impact of one variable over the other*. When we are interested in finding *only in relationship* and the *direction of the relationship* (is advertisement expenditure increasing or decreasing and sales increasing or decreasing) then we are talking about *correlation*. If we are further interested in measuring the *impact of one over another* e.g. How much sales are affected by advertisement expenditure then we are talking about *causality* (study regression analysis and ANOVA analysis when you complete your syllabus to get a deeper insight into the subject research methodology). Experimental designs *(Experimental design* is a type of quantitative research which often uses causal research structure *e.g. A clinical trial of desprin medicine for a headache)* will become part of it.

Seeing all the three different types of research do not think that they will work in isolation. They all can be combined to satisfy the purpose of the study, just like Anand (2016) did for her work on loneliness (See the citation at the end of the book and visit the website www.shodganga. com for more details on different types of research used by researchers).

Do not get confused with the types of research design we used. Actually, we see them as the two sides of the same coin. You can see research work as:

- Exploratory Research, Descriptive Research & Causal Research (Blumberg, B., Cooper, D. R., & Schindler, P. S., 2005), or,

- *On the basis of approaches or strategies of inquiry:* Experimental, Correlation & Survey Research (Quantitative Research); Grounded Theory, Ethnographic, Narrative (Qualitative Research); and Concurrent, Sequential, embedded and transformative (Mixed Method) as defined by Creswell (2017).

1.14 Validity in Experiment: Internal and External Validity

Two important concepts of measurement are required to be studied in experimental research. One is *reliability* and the other is *validity*.

Reliability is a property of an experiment which shows that the experiment design is faithful. *A measure is said to be reliable if on different attempts the experiment produces the same result* (Zikmund, Babin, & Carr, 2009). One core property which can be defined by the definition of reliability is consistency i.e. how much consistent the system is.

Validity in an experiment refers to the degree to which *the design (variables, instruments, methods) is able to measure its underlying concept.* The quality of an experiment is judged by the degree to which it satisfies two types of validity.

Internal validity: It is about the accuracy of the variables, samples in predicting the desired outcome *e.g. Accuracy of using cigarette smoking among tobacco variable in predicting lung cancer.*

External validity: When the results drawn from an experiment is validated in the real-world setting, we say that the experiment is high on external validity. External validity is increased when the sample is a representative of the population (Zikmund, Babin, & Carr, 2009) and when the results can be generalized to the much broader area (Creswell, 2017) like that for other peoples, different market segment etc. If the experiment which can successfully measure the difference between groups, can be utilized to measure difference within groups, we can say that the experiment is high on validity.

Introduction to Business Research, Research Process **25**

1.15 Secondary Data Research

Secondary data research means the res*earch work done on the basis of the secondary data source.* Let us begin with defining the term 'Data'.

All the information present in the external world is data. Your family members information is a type of data, the number of girlfriends and boyfriends you are having is again a data. "Data is ubiquitous" (*Found this phrase in a course on Exploratory Data Analysis Using R (2019) by Facebook on in.udacity.com*).

You need data to fulfill your research objectives e.g. if your research objective is to find out advertisement impact on sales then you need data on two variables advertisement and sales because then only you can measure the impact of one variable over other. In a business context, all the information related to the business world is data as we can use it for future use. e.g. The sales of the past three years of a company is data.

Data can be collected from two broad sources. *Primary source* and a *secondary source.*

All the data that is collected first hand i.e. *the data collected by you specific to your research is a primary data* e.g. you interviewing the general manager of a company or you collecting data through a survey in a shopping mall. Whereas, all the data which is required by you but has *not been collected by you* is the secondary data source for your study.eg. the books, magazines, articles you refer for your project is a secondary data. We will cover the primary data in detail later. Let us start with secondary data first as it is as per your CBCS pattern.

As mentioned all the data that has been collected and/or presented by someone else is a *secondary data.*eg. Newspaper, magazines, journal articles, company newsletters, government reports etc. are all examples of secondary data. It is not the data collected in the first hand by you.

1.15.1 Secondary Data Advantages and Disadvantages

The advantages of secondary data include: Its availability; less expensive in comparison to primary data; is presented more often in a structured

26 A Concise Handbook of Business Research

form, saves time, money and energy, when primary data could not be collected, some data can only best be studied using secondary data *e.g. Financial performs ratios.*

The disadvantages of secondary data include: Data may be outdated considering your research, it can be incomplete for your research, the unit of measurement may be different because of which it can be more time consuming.

1.15.2 Criteria for Evaluating Secondary Sources

Evaluating secondary data is an important task. Zikmund, Babin, & Carr (2009) suggest few questions, to be answered by the researcher while evaluating secondary data sources:

- Do the data apply to the population of interest?
- Do the data apply to the time period of interest?
- Do the secondary data appear in the correct units of measurement?
- Do the data cover the subject of interest in adequate detail?

Answering these questions will certainly going to help you because with this you can fit the right data source for your study. If the source you selected is not fitting into your study, leave it and move to another secondary data source.

1.15.3 Secondary Data Sources in the Indian Context

As mentioned, some of the core secondary data sources include *Newspaper, magazines, journal articles, company newsletters and reports, government reports and websites, documents from other websites.* Let us explore some of them in the Indian context

You can get these sources either in electronic format or in hard copy. So make sure in which format your secondary data source is available.

- **Newspapers:** Articles and published data in Times of India, Hindustan Times, Economic Times, Business Line, Business Standard.

Introduction to Business Research, Research Process **27**

- **Magazines:** Articles and published data in Business India, Business today, The Franchising world, Forbes India, India Today, PCQuest, Times Magazines Asia, The Week.

- **Journal articles:** For journal article important databases comes from international databases, which includes: www.scopus.com, www.emeraldinsight.com, www.elsevier.com , www.ebsco.com, www.ssrn.com.

- In Indian context you can log onto to the individual university websites (for more information on list of universities log on to www.ugc.ac.in, a university governing body portal) for online journals for e.g. you can log onto http://www.gkv.ac.in/?page_id = 1252 or www.gurukulbusinessreview.in, to access my department, **Faculty of Management Studies, Gurukula kangri University** annually published journal, Gurukul Business Review (GBR).

- **Company Newsletters and Reports:** The reports and newsletters are published by companies. Some are published with a fixed frequency like that of annual reports and some are occasional, like that of special reports and newsletters. These reports are available in electronic format in the company websites or can be taken in hard copy from company offices. For e.g. you can have ONGC company annual report from the website: http://www.ongcindia. com/wps/wcm/connect/ongcindia/Home/Performance/Annual_ Reports/.An e.g. of a newsletter can be taken from https://www. icicilombard.com/newsletter.

- **Government Reports:** Government reports are reports which are available from the portals of government or from the government office. Go to www.gov.in and you can get a huge amount of information and reports in the Indian context. You can also get information which is state specific e.g. if you want to have information about Uttarakhand state (from where we belong) log on to http://uk.gov.in/

28   A Concise Handbook of Business Research

- **Documents from other websites:** For Ph.D. thesis, you can also log into http://shodhganga.inflibnet.ac.in/, which is a database of the thesis from universities all over India. Here you can get many Ph.D. theses for your topic.

  You can also log into the national digital library a government of India initiative in collaboration with IIT Kharagpur for many digital reports and material at https://ndl.iitkgp.ac.in

1.16 Syndicate Research

Syndicated Research is research funded by market research companies and the results of such research are made available to everyone who wishes to purchase it. This research is conducted by market research organizations for various purpose some of them are: *updating particular market knowledge, establishing itself as a market research firm, to satisfy their own client needs* (Verma, 2013).

E.g. Of the companies involved in syndicate research are *Syndicate research limited (SRL)*, which provides in-depth research on all trading organizations operating in the Lloyd's (world's specialist insurance market) of London insurance market (www.syndicateresearch.com, 2018). US-based research firm *Nielsen* is another example of a firm involved in syndicate research (http://global.shopnielsen.com/reports/region-india, 2018).

In the Indian context, three firms are more visible in syndicate research work: *IMRB International, Majestic MRSS, RNB Research*. Do visit the company websites for more information.

Tentative Exam Questions

1. Explain the nature and scope of business research.
2. Research has an important role in business decision making. Explain.
3. In what areas of business, research have its applications?

Introduction to Business Research, Research Process **29**

4. Explain the research process in detail.
5. What is the difference between management research problem and the business research problem?
6. Explain, how a problem can be formulated from real-world to the research world?
7. Define Research Design. Explain the key ingredients of the research design.
8. What do you mean by validity in experimental design? Differentiate between internal and external validity?
9. Define secondary data. How it is different from primary data?
10. What are the good sources of secondary data? Explain their advantages and disadvantages.
11. Secondary data is present in the internet world. What criterion should be used to evaluate the secondary data source?
12. What is 'Shodhganga' and for what purpose it is used?
13. What is Syndicated Research? Explain the working of any syndicate research company you know.

❑❑❑

2

Primary Data Research and Its Tools and Techniques

> **Syllabus Unit 2:** *Primary Data Collection: Survey Vs. Observations. Random sample collection method, Comparison of self-administered, telephone, mail, emails techniques and qualitative research tools.*

2.1 Primary Data

A data collected to be called as primary data should satisfy two conditions: One, It should be collected first hand by you for your research work e.g. the data you collect on company performance by interviewing the general manager of a company) and two, it should not be a published data of someone else.

The primary data comes handy when the objective of the researcher is to add new insight into the problem. It is also supposed to remove any biases (*any association among variables developed due to past data evidence)* developed by using secondary data collected in the past. Say, for an example a secondary data published in the 1970s in a journal says that the consumers did not like computers because they were too heavy to carry, however, the statement may not be true in present context as the size due to the development in the technology has already reduced a lot.

(31)

2.1.1 Collecting Primary Data: Survey, Observation, and Interview

Depending upon the nature of the problem, set objectives, and the topic under study you can make out what data type will more suit your study. For deeper insight, you may require both quantitative and qualitative data for your study.

When confirmed that you need to collect primary data you need to know the methods used for collecting primary data.

Broadly, there are two **methods of data collection** in the business research context, one is *observation* and the other one is *communicate* (Blumberg, Cooper, & Schindler, 2005), which means getting in touch with your participants. In communicate category we can collect primary data using two methods using *questionnaires and interview*. So overall, we can say that we have three methods of primary data collection:
1. Questionnaire method
2. Interview method
3. Observation method

The first two methods of primary data collection come under *survey methods* as defined in most of the books for e.g. in (Zikmund, Babin, & Carr, 2009). Let us elaborate on them.

2.1.2 Survey Methods: Questionnaire and Interview Method

Questionnaire Method

It is one of the common methods of primary data collection. In this, the researcher asks participants about their opinions and behaviors and get the answers recorded using a questionnaire. Depending on the expertise and needs of the researcher the questions to be used for measuring opinions or behaviors can be **close-ended** like for e.g. do you like a product x (yes or no), or the questionnaire can be **open-ended** for e.g. which product you like the most (x or y) and why? ………. In open-ended types of questions, the researcher does not define boundaries and the participant is free to express his feeling like that for the product in the question above.

Interview Method

In the interview method of data collection, the researcher collects the first-hand information from the participant by asking questions regarding his experience on the problem under investigation e.g. suppose your study is on knowing the level of work stress among bank employees, in interview method, you may sit *one-on-one* with selected bank employees, or you may ask your questions to a *group of employees* by making them sit at a commonplace to know about their work stress. The first method is a *face to face* or an in-depth interview method (A qualitative survey method), whereas the latter is a *focused group interview method* (again a qualitative data collection method).

However, at times the location of the participant is too far away for the above two methods, in this case you can conduct a telephonic interview to get the responses to your questions. In summary, there are three methods for conducting an interview: face to face, focused group, and telephonic (Wilson, 2014)

2.1.3 Observation Method

As the name suggests the observation method is about observing and recording the variables under investigation e.g. observing consumer behavior in a shopping mall or observing the behavior of doctors in a hospital. Observation includes *monitoring behaviors* e.g. Non-verbal analysis, linguistic analysis, spatial or distance relationship analysis, and non behavioural activities and *conditions*, for e.g. record analysis, physical condition analysis and physical process analysis (Blumberg, Cooper, & Schindler, 2005).

Observation is about sensing the background information and the information which is present in hand. You might have heard from your teachers saying that the AICTE team is coming for an inspection. One of the methods which they will be using to evaluate your college performance will be the observation method. We relate this method more with the qualitative methodology (*where we think we need to interact with the participants in physical*) than with quantitative methodology (*where we think that interacting with participants will create a mess rather than anything else, so be separated for analysis*).

Types of Observations Methods

In books, you will find an observation method categorized as:

- Direct or Indirect observation (Blumberg, Cooper, & Schindler, 2005)
- Participant or Nonparticipant observation (Wilson, 2014)

In *Direct observation*, the observer is physically present and he himself monitor the task at hand. Whereas in *Indirect observation* recording is done using a mechanical or electronic device e.g. a camera in a shopping mall. Indirect observation is required in some situations because your interaction can disturb the setting.

In participant observation, the researcher interacts and becomes part of the group under study e.g. the ethnographic researchers. You might have seen in the national geographic or the discovery channel, where one heroic person resides in a village to sense the village peoples believes and culture. Whereas, in nonparticipant observation, the researcher remains separated from the group under study e.g. a researcher trying to find out cultural differences by survey method using a predefined questionnaire.

You can see that both classifications are supporting one another. Looks more like the two sides of the same coin.

2.2 Random Sample Collection Method

The term random sample is related to the random sampling method which is covered in unit three of this book, it is present in detail there.

2.3 Survey vs Observations

Hope the definitions of both the survey and observation method are clear to you. Do one thing, write a comparison and get it checked by your class teacher.

2.4 Comparison of Self-Administered, Telephone, Mail, e-mails Techniques

Self-administered techniques means you are talking about a questionnaire or an interview method. However, at times you have to use a telephone, or an email as a medium. Now think, *when should you meet your respondents face to face, and when should you go for telephonic conversation, or emails for data collection?*

Self-administered techniques are best suited for studies in which it is easy to assess the participants and the *research site* is under the researcher's control. Where the participant is sitting at a distant location, meeting every participant is not an easy task.

Time and cost will play an important role in your study. The more you get physically involved, the more you have to cover physical location, the more time and cost will be involved.

Email and telephone calls are best suited for situations where your *respondent is busy, fixing the meeting in the office is difficult* (when the individual time is not fixed), contacting *corporate offices (*which generally are at important and big cities), or the respondent is at a *distant location* where it is not easy to approach. The corporate offices are formal structures so you need permission to meet them, here emails and telephonic conversations (to start the conversation process) are recommended. Both structures have their own advantages and disadvantages.

1. In comparison to self-administered, emails and telephonic conversations are subjected to disturbances and communication errors. So, make sure you do a proper homework before moving onto it.
2. Time and cost will play an important role and can make one advantageous and one disadvantageous.
3. If your questionnaire is lengthy, self-administered is recommended.
4. The internet-based structure should be used when the sample size is very large.

36 A Concise Handbook of Business Research

5. The response rate is low for internet or telephonic based data collection than personal administration (Zikmund, Babin, & Carr, 2009).

2.5 Which Method to Use in a Study

The method you choose for your study will depend on the following factors:

1. **Your Learnings and Belief About the World Around You:** The method to choose for your data collection will depend upon your learning and experience from the world around you. Creswell (2014) has called it a worldview whereas Crotty (The foundation of social research: Meaning and perspective in the research process, 1998) has explained it in two words: epistemology and ontology. For your consideration, you need to know that there are two explanations of the world around you. One which can be felt by being more separated from the world, just like a scientist working in a more unbiased manner. Whereas the other belief is about being part of the world around you, like a researcher on human culture. If you think to study a problem you need to be part of the problem, you are more subjective as per ontological view and constructive as per epistemological view. In this case, you will choose methods which help to interact with the participants like the **interview or participant observation method** in your study. Whereas if you think the problem under consideration needs to be studied more in an objective manner, an unbiased manner, then you are having an objective ontological view and post positive epistemology view. In this case, you may choose a **questionnaire method or nonparticipant observation method**. To master the concept read the cited books.

2. **The Complexity and Nature of The Problem:** The more complex the problem is, the more you may need primary and secondary data for your study. The researcher working on the

complex issues where we need to collect both primary data and secondary data to study the problem falls in pragmatic worldview as per epistemology, and will include both the subjective and objective ontological view to study the problem. As per this view, the researchers of this field put the problem at the center to carry out their study.

3. **The Amount of Hard Work You Want to Do:** Using more data sources will make you sweat. So, make sure if you are ready to work hard enough then only choose more methods of data collections to study your problem.

4. **If The Data is Already Available and is Sufficient for Your study:** In this case, it is better to use secondary literature than primary data because the data is already available.

5. **Some Data are Available in Published Form:** The financial data like company ROE, ROA or profit are available on the company websites, important websites like *www.moneycontrol.com,* so you can use them directly for your research.

Tentative Exam Questions

1. Explain the different primary data collection methods in detail.
2. What is sampling? Explain random sampling.
3. Make a comparison of self-administered, telephone, emails techniques on the basis of their use in the field of research.

3

Measurement, Scaling and Sampling

Syllabus Unit 03: UNIT-III: Measurement & Scaling: Primary scales of Measurement-Nominal, Ordinal, and Interval & Ratio. Scaling techniques-paired comparison, rank order, constant sum, semantic differential, itemized ratings, Likert Scale; Questionnaire-form & design. Fundamentals of scale evaluation-Reliability, Validity and Generalizability, Sampling: Sampling techniques, determination of sample size using statistical techniques. Cronbach alpha test for reliability (Using Software).

3.1 Concept of Measurement

Assigning a numerical value to a variable such that it can be quantified is measurement (Weiers, 2008). *Now what does it mean and how is it useful?* Let us understand with the help of an example. Try to measure the body fever by a thermometer, and without a thermometer only by the touch of your hand on the forehead. By touch, it is hard to tell the exact number, whereas with the help of thermometer we are able to identify whether we should go to the doctor or not. If the temperature is, say more than 100.5 degree Celsius, we can say it is the time to go to the doctor. Just by measuring we are able to link and measure the variable well (In this case fever in the body).

(39)

3.2 Concept of Scaling

We all use a ruler generally to draw a straight line. It tells us the length of the object which is being measured or the object we are measuring is longer or shorter than another object.

Scaling concept is drawn from a ruler. Fitting the variables with the help of questions on scale helps us to measure it quantitatively,

e.g. Do girls like chocolates?

– Disagree	Neutral	Agree
+1	0	-1

Just by clicking at any of the options we can find out the opinion of an individual, and if 1,00,000 girls click on it and say agree, then the data can be of importance to the company like Nestle.

3.3 Scales of Measurement

In research, to measure a variable following scale are available:

Nominal Scale: In business research, this scale is used to *categorize variables* and is generally visible in the initial part of the questionnaire in a survey. For e.g., If you want to know how many males and females participated in your survey or whether the employee who is filling your questionnaire is from public sector bank, private sector bank or foreign bank, you will be using a nominal scale. You can have two, three, four or as many categories your objective wants for the categorization of data. In summary, to measure the variable with categorical data like color, gender, segment, a nominal scale is used.

Ordinal Scale: This scale is an upgradation of the nominal scale with some added features. When the objective is not only to categorize variables but also to produce a *rank* among them, then we use an ordinal scale. In this one item is of a higher order than other, e.g. If you ask your friend or your survey respondents to give a rank one to the toothpaste you use the most, and rank five to the toothpaste you use least, from five different kinds of toothpaste, is an example of ordinal scale.

Measurement, Scaling and Sampling **41**

Interval Scale: The third scale is the interval scale, which is a numeric scale, and is the one which can do more than nominal and ordinal work. This scale has the property of order as well as distance. It has a meaningful mathematical difference but does not have a true zero (www.surveymonkey.com, 2019). Here 'true zero' means that zero still means something *e.g. if you say that the temperature is '0' degree it does not mean that temperature does not exist, it is still there, this time it is zero degree.*

Mathematical operations like addition, subtraction, finding mean and standard deviation, are done on this scale (Panneerselvam, 2012) . Examples of this scale include your temperature, time and date, as they all can be studied as interval data. If designed well can be used for measuring perception and opinion (*Visit surveymoney.com, here you will find different survey style questions*). Statistical tests can be done on this scale.

Ratio Scale: It is a scale which contains the property of all the three scales mentioned above plus one unique property which other scales do not have i.e. *it has a true meaningful zero.* This scale is used in measuring continuous variables (continuous variables are those which can take infinite values between any two points (support.minitab, 2017)) like *length, breadth, weight, volume* etc.

Just to summarize when the objective of measurement is to categorize, we will use a nominal scale (male vs female). When the objective is to rank a variable or different variable, we use a rank scale. If the objective is to find out the difference between two intervals of continuous nature or if you want to measure data such that you will need, mean, standard deviation or combination of these to understand your data, we will use interval scale. But this scale does not have a true zero. Whereas if the objective is to measure continuous variables and we want to have a true zero in the scale we will use ratio scale.

3.4 Scaling Techniques for Measurement

Scaling techniques mean fitting the questions in a questionnaire such that the opinions of the respondent can be measured to perfection. We saw different methods of measuring a variable above. Now let us put the variables in the questionnaire. When it comes to the development of scale we have many options depending on what you want to measure. The scales we choose to measure variables under study can broadly be categorized into a *Ranking* and *Rating scale*.

Ranking Scales are used to measure the variable under study which includes comparison and ranking. The scales which falls in this category are *Paired Comparisons* (generates preference or rank or order), *Forced Choice* (order or rank), *Comparative Scale* (preference to a point of reference).

Rating Scale, on the other hand, is the one having several response categories and are used to measure the variables without any comparison or developing a rank. The scales which falls under this category are *Dichotomous scale* (like yes or no response), *Category Scale* (male or female), if you have not forgotten a type of nominal scales. *Likert Scale* (strongly agree to strongly which is more disagree), a type of interval/ratio scale depending on the use, *Numerical Scale, Semantic Differential Scale, Itemized Rating Scale, Stapel Scale, Graphic Rating Scale, Consensus Scale,* again types of interval scales, *Fixed or Constant Sum Rating Scale*, more a type of ordinal scale.

Let us discuss few rating and ranking scales as per your syllabus.

Paired Comparison: In this scaling technique we present the respondent with two objects and ask him to pick the preferred object, e.g. you prefer soap 'A' brand or Soap 'B' brand for washing clothes. We may use more than two objects but comparisons are made in pairs.

Rank Order: The e.g. of this type of scale is forced choice scale. This scale enables respondents to rank objects relative to one another, among the alternatives provided. This is easier for the respondents, particularly if the number of choices to be ranked is limited in number.

Measurement, Scaling and Sampling **43**

Constant Sum: In this scale, we give fixed weight to an item (say out of 100) and then ask respondents to put his preference in weights such that the total sum cannot be more than the constant sum we fixed. e.g. If you want to measure the beauty of a flower on say four characteristics: color, leaf length, size, and you will give weights such that the total sum is not more than 100. You might give 60 to color, 10 to leaf length, 30 to lower size. This scale is quite useful in measuring the attributes of an object (Sekaran, 2003).

Semantic Differential: It is used for measuring the meaning of things and concepts. Here 'meaning' denotes to strength, value or activity (scaling, n.d.) inherited by the object not by its name but by its strength. This scale is used to derive attitude, opinion or values towards an object. e.g. Rate Shri. Narendra Modi as a prime minister on the points below is an example of semantic differential scale. It uses a 05-07-point scale with two poles measuring opposite reactions. Three key bipolar adjectives found by Osgood (1964) and used for measuring semantic difference is mentioned below.

Strong	___:___:___:___:___:___	Weak
Good	___:___:___:___:___:___	Bad
Active	___:___:___:___:___:___	Passive

Itemized Ratings: A 5-point or 7-point scale with anchors, as needed, is provided for each item and the respondent states the appropriate number on the side of each item, or circles the relevant number against each item. The responses to the items are then summated. This uses an interval scale.

Likert Scale: A scale having 05 points of measurement. Which starts with strongly disagree, Disagree, Neither Agree nor Disagree, Agree and Strongly agree. The scale has two types of construction: Having values 1,2,3,4,5, where 1 starts with strongly disagree, 2 -disagree, 3-Neighter agree or disagree, 4-agree, 5-strongly. The other is by having value -2, -1, 0, +1, +2. The measurement goes either by summing the values of the respondent or taking the values as an average, interpretable in the form of scale values. This scale is the most common and easy to use for measuring attitude, opinion of the respondents. You generally use it as an

44 A Concise Handbook of Business Research

interval ratio scale if you are interested in making interpretations of your sample on the basis of mean and std. deviation. Statement construction plays a key role in the Likert scale.

3.5 Questionnaire-Form & Design

Among different forms of data collection methods, we know that one of the methods is through a questionnaire (if you have forgotten the others, please revise chapter 2). Generally, a questionnaire contains many sets of questions to extract information about the respondents. It contains some nominal questions like Male or Female, Salary Range, Types of banks etc. It contains some ordinal questions if you want to rank one object in comparison to others. It contains some interval or ratio scale questions to have a range of opinions of the respondents. Depending on the objective of the study the questionnaire will take its shape.

As far as the types of questions used in a questionnaire, we can classify questions into three broad categories. One, having close-ended questions like the few mentioned above or it can be an open-ended question where we give full chance to the respondent to express his views on the issue or object. The third category is of mixed method questions which are a combination of both in a single questionnaire. Let us elaborate.

Having Close-ended Questions: In these types of questions you bound the respondent to answer according to your preference.eg. Like that in a Likert scale, by asking an opinion of a respondent from strongly agree to strongly disagree., e.g. I love playing basketball:

Strongly Disagree ( )   Disagree ( ) Indecisive   ( )   Agree ( ) Strongly agree   ( ).

Having Open-ended Questions: In this type of questions, you do not bound the respondent to answer according to you i.e. The respondent is free to express his opinion on the question, e.g. Why do think the present government should stay for 10 years? ....
....
....
....

Measurement, Scaling and Sampling **45**

Having mixed questions: These types of questions are used when either of the above two forms of questions alone are not able to satisfy our objective or will not be able to provide the complete answer to the desired question.

3.5.1 Mode of Presenting a Questionnaire

We take either of the two forms of a questionnaire to reach our respondents: Electronic and printed questionnaire. The data of your respondents can be collected either by printing it in hard copy and get it filled by the respondent or by developing on the platform like google. doc on the internet and sending it electronically through email. You can also send your hard copy of the questionnaire designed to the respondent by scanning it in images making it a '.jpeg' file and sending it through email. The respondent then may reply by sending you the scanned copy of the completely filled questionnaire.

3.5.2 Important Points on Questionnaire Design

1. The questionnaire should start with 'About The Questionnaire' i.e. describing the purpose of the questionnaire.

2. The questionnaire should express the importance of the data to be collected .

3. The privacy of the respondent should not be compromised (If required). For this, you may require proper coding from your side.

4. The questionnaire should contain a section on demographic details (age, income, gender, designation etc.) of the respondents. It helps us to find out the characteristic of the sample from which we filled data. For e.g., after collecting 200 respondents data for your study you may find out that 150 were males and only 50 were females. Generally, it is placed in the initial part of the format. However few researchers like to put it at the end of the questionnaire.

5. The questionnaire contains only those questions which directly measures your variables. If you are carrying any questions which

46 A Concise Handbook of Business Research

are not directly related to your study, remove it. Get it thoroughly checked by your supervisor or class teacher. During pilot testing, you will get lots of help from them to improve your questionnaire. So make sure you don't skip this process.

6. Try to connect your questions in the logical order (Wilson, 2014).

7. Try to have a concise questionnaire. Especially in electronic format, the extended questions can cause a problem for e.g. Seeing a two-page electronic questionnaire can demotivate a respondent from replying. Here concise means a minimum set of questions required for successful work completion.

8. At the bottom of the questionnaire give space for name and signature of the respondent. Make it optional if you feel the respondent will be unwilling to respond to your questionnaire because of this. You can make it at the top of the questionnaire also in the demographic details section.

9. Attach a covering letter to your questionnaire. It should contain the information about you, your work and its connection with the respondent. If your questionnaire is already lengthy then you can put point 2. and point 3. above in the covering letter in detail and in summary in your questionnaire.

Now let us give you some real-world examples of questionnaire format. We are mentioning a few links from the Indian Ph.D. thesis Database (a secondary source of the database if you remember!) http://shodhganga.inflibnet.ac.in/.

Link 1:

http://shodhganga.inflibnet.ac.in/handle/10603/88960

This is the link to the questionnaire of (Guda Vasudeva, 2016) Ph.D. thesis work from IIM Indore.

Link 2:

http://shodhganga.inflibnet.ac.in/handle/10603/28369

This is the link to the questionnaire of (Dangi, 2012) Ph.D. thesis work from the Department of Management Studies, University of Delhi.

The reason for mentioning Ph.D. questionnaires is the standard of the format used by the researchers during their study.

3.6 Fundamentals of Scale Evaluation

The fundamentals of scale evaluation in a simple sense mean- making sure that your questionnaire is effective enough to measure the problem under study. It has to pass two tests before you run in mass to your respondents and has to pass one test for making sure that it can be used with the same precision over to some other population. Reliability and Validity are the tests related to the first point and Generalizability is related to the other. (Example to understand the concept of generalizability can be the Classical Conditioning Theory which was applied and tested on dogs (where we ring bell and dog starts carving) and its results were equally applicable to human being learnings. Let us see them in detail.

3.6.1 Reliability

Reliability: In simple language, it is an indicator of internal consistency of the measuring instrument, your questionnaire. A measure is reliable when different attempts at measuring something repeatedly produces the same result (i.e. the instrument is internally consistent). *Coefficient alpha (α)*, also known as *Cronbach alpha*, is a sign by which you represent reliability in statistics. A good alpha value is above .80. However, if it is between .65 and .80, it is still considered a satisfactory value. (Goforth, 2015).

Split-half method is used for assessing internal consistency. It performs by checking the results of one-half of a set of scaled items against the results from the other half of the scaled items. It represents the average of all possible split-half reliabilities for a construct. In a simple sense, it is the extent to which the scale measures one underlying factor or construct. Another method which is used for measuring reliability is the *Test-Retest method* which administers the same scale or measure to the same respondents at two separate points in time to test for stability.

48 A Concise Handbook of Business Research

3.6.2 Validity

A good instrument should have these two key characteristics one, it should be consistent and two, it should be accurate. Reliability discussed earlier was related to consistency of the instrument, whereas the word validity is related to the accuracy of the instrument. Accuracy is about asking two questions to self, *"Is the instrument I am using, able to measure what it is meant for?"*, *"can it cover and measure the desired concept?"*. It is about hitting the center of the bat every time you hit a ball. Validity is the accuracy of a measuring instrument.

The six basic types of validity to be watched for maintaining accuracy are:

Face Validity is an extent to which a procedure, test or research instrument is covering the concept subjectivity for which it has been designed. It is about getting a confirmation from the experts, e.g. if the ten bank managers say that your questionnaire on banking services is good and able to meet the problem under consideration, then it means your instrument face validity sounds good. In a simple sense, it logically reflects what your research instrument supposed to do.

Content Validity refers to the degree to which your instrument measures and covers the domain of interest. It is about asking to self, *"Do the items used in the instrument captures the entire scope?"*, *"Is it inside the boundaries for measuring the problem?"*. Content validity is deeper than face validity.

Criterion Validity refers to the practical exposure of the instrument and its outcome. According to Zikmund, Babin, & Carr (2009), it is about addressing the question, *"How well does my instrument work in practice?"*. (Also read concurrent and Predictive validity).

Convergent Validity is a property of a highly reliable scale. It is about having different concepts in the instrument but highly related just like we have all body parts of the bicycle (e.g. tires, tube, breaks) very different from that of the bike.

Discriminant Validity represents how unique or distinct is a measure (Zikmund , Babin , & Carr , 2009). In a sense, an instrument should have highly related body parts just like the by cycle, but it does not mean we can have tyres replaced by breaks. The concepts or the themes measuring concept should be related but not overly related, that is they should discriminate e.g. when we talk about measuring human resource management of an organization, we can have broad themes like Recruitment and Selection Policy, Induction, Performance Appraisal, Training & Development, and Maintenance. They are all related to human resource management of an organization but they are different from one another as a concept or a theme.

Construct Validity: It exists when a measure reliably measures and truthfully represents a unique concept(s). It includes all the above discussed: Face validity, Content validity, Criterion validity, Convergent validity, Discriminant validity.

Multivariate procedures like factor analysis can be useful in establishing construct validity.

3.6.3 Generalizability

It means how much the measuring instrument remains consistent in different situations. for e.g. If a questionnaire which was used to predict the behavior of MBA boys is used to predict the behavior of BCA boys, and the reliability and validity come good, we say that the instrument generalizability is good, and can also be used for measuring the concept with other populations.

3.7 Sampling

Before understanding the term sample, let me define the term **population** (sometimes called as the universe) for a researcher. A *population* is a complete collection of elements about which we wish to make some interpretation (better to use a word inference in place of interpretation) e.g. populations of India is somewhere more than 120 crores, the total number of students in my BBA class are 60, the total number of students in my MBA class is 45. etc.

50 A Concise Handbook of Business Research

But the term population takes shape depending upon the definition, narrowness, or broadness of our problem. E.g. The total students in our BBA class are 60 makes one population and in the MBA class are 50 makes another population. But If we want to study the students behavior in our present institution, FMS, GKV, then the population of both class automatically gets added to 110 as now we are talking about the total students and not for a single class.

3.7.1 Sample

At times when the population is big enough to be studied, we try to extract some elements of the population such that the problem can be studied. But the most important factor in choosing the elements from the population is that the number of elements chosen should together constitute the same characteristics as that of a population (accuracy of a sample). We call this chosen group of elements as a *sample* (e.g. a mug of water from a bucket.) and the process of choosing the samples as *sampling*. Now every unit which is in the sample is called as the *sampling unit*.

One important term which you should take into consideration while dealing with sampling is *sampling error*, which is the error generated due to observed samples and not studying population. As sample size increases sampling error deceases.

3.7.2 Sampling Techniques

As mentioned above, a sample is a small portion of a population we would like to measure. This portion chosen for measurement is supposed to be representative of the population which due to time, budget, the population being large, and other constraints we are not able to measure. The process of choosing the samples as we know is called sampling.

We can define sampling under two broad classifications:

- Probability Sampling and Non-Probability sampling and
- Proportionate and Nonproportionate sampling.

Probability Sampling and Non-Probability Sampling

When each population element in the population has an equal chance of being selected as a sample unit, is known as probability sampling. Whereas, when the sample unit is selected on the basis of the judgment of an expert or with some intentional biases, the sampling is called nonprobability sampling.

Under **Probability Sampling** we have many methods to choose samples:

Simple Random Sampling: In this type of sampling method each element in the population has an equal chance of being selected in the sampling unit. Though it is more statistically sound, it is the toughest one because the randomness may call for a sample from different regions. E.g. if you want to choose 50 bank branches samples from India, and do it using simple random sampling, you may get sampling units from all over India which at times are hard to catch. But still, it is the best as far as statistics is concerned.

There are Two Basic Methods of Random Sampling

(*a*) Using random number table; In this, you list the item in population in some serial order. Then you assign a number to it by seeing the random table. For more see you statistics book.

(*b*) Using MS-Excel software to generate a random number. Use command RAND ( ) for using random sampling. You can see some videos of it on www.youtube.com

Systematic Sampling: As the name suggests it follows a certain systematic selection of sample units. In this, we select a starting point by a random process and then every nth number on the list is selected e.g. choosing the first sample randomly using above-mentioned process and then selecting every 5th or every 20th Item in the population.

Stratified Sampling: It is a sampling procedure in which we divide the population on the basis of some characteristics (called as strata). E.g. gender, age, class, or income, and then we perform simple random sampling in each stratum. One of the basic objectives of it is to get a sample size with equal proportion to say for e.g. Male and female in

52 A Concise Handbook of Business Research

a population is 70:30 then by stratified sampling you divide the population into males and females. And then you can choose 70% of males from the first strata and 30% of females from the second strata. A stratum is homogeneous inside and differ from other strata.

Cluster Sampling: A cluster is heterogeneous inside and similar outside. E.g. If the objective is to find out malnutrition children in say Uttarakhand, we can select the districts in which the rate of malnutrition among children is high. For e.g. we can take Haridwar district and Kotdwar. Then we can randomly select the participants from each district.

The higher version of cluster sampling is multistage cluster sampling. For e.g. after selecting Haridwar as a district, we can then choose different blocks in each district, say for e.g. bahadrabad and Haridwar city region, and then randomly select the samples from each district. It is economical and efficient especially when the population size is large.

Non-Probability Sampling Methods

When we remove the concept of randomness from sampling and try to get sampling units on the basis of some judgment, convenience, referencing, we are talking about Non-Probability sampling. Let see the methods under it in detail.

Convenience Sampling: it is a sampling procedure for obtaining those people or units that are most conveniently available or are willing to participate in the study.

Judgment (Purposive) Sampling: Under this technique, an experienced individual selects the samples based on a personal judgment about some appropriate characteristic of the population under study. The researcher experience and a strong reason to use some particular samples for study form the basis for this sampling, e.g. choosing stock brokers/ analyst for a TV show by a business news channel.

Snowball Sampling: It is a procedure of sample selection in which initial respondents are selected by any probability methods discussed

Measurement, Scaling and Sampling **53**

above and then additional respondents are obtained from information provided by the initial respondents. It is more a sort of reference sampling. It is widely used for online surveys where sample size is large.

Quota Sampling: It is a nonprobability version of stratified sampling. First, you make a strata (a collection of sampling units is homogeneous by some characteristics in one stratum than the other) and then choose samples using any of the above methods. *e.g. choosing sample based on some age group (formation of strata), and then using judgment sampling further (purposeful selection).*

Proportional versus Disproportional Sampling

In proportionate sampling, the sampling units drawn from each stratum is in proportion, e.g. we discussed that in stratified random sampling.

Whereas under disproportionate sampling sample size for each stratum is allocated according to analytical considerations. In short when you require an equal proportion of population then we use proportionate sampling else we use disproportionate sampling.

Use them in line with probability and nonprobability sampling structure.

3.7.3 Determination of Sample Size

Among different methods to look for the required sample size we will discuss three:

1. Referring to a ready-made sample table
2. Estimating sample size based on the number of items in the scale.
3. Rough Estimate (Creswell, 2017)

Sample Table

Sample size can be determined using a sample table (created on the basis of the mathematical formula used for calculating sample size). It is a readymade way of choosing a sample size. For discussion, we have referred a sample table from an online resource, https://www.research-advisors.com/tools/SampleSize.htm. Here we are presenting a discussion on how to use it. Take a print out of the table from the website and see this section further.

54 A Concise Handbook of Business Research

1. We got two confidence intervals 95% and 99% with four margin of error, population size and the respective sample size (see table 3.1). It means when we take a particular sample size for a given population size mentioned in the table, in one situation we are considering the results to be produced with 5% of error chance, wherein another situation results will be produced with only 1% of error chance. E.g., For population size of 30, with 95% confidence, 5% margin of error, the sample size will be 28.

Table. 3.1: Reading Sample Size Table

Population size	Confidence = 95% Margin of Error				Confidence = 99% Margin of Error			
	5.0%	3.5%	2.5%	1.0%	5.0%	3.5%	2.5%	1.0%
10	10	10	10	10	10	10	10	10
20	19	20	20	20	19	20	20	20
30	28	29	29	30	28	29	29	30

Source: https://www.research-advisors.com/tools/SampleSize.htm

2. As the population size increases from 50,000 to 5,00,000 (see table 3.2), sample size also increases, but grows at a slower pace. But differ for 5% and 3.5 % error margin (what we call as **sampling error**). However, as you keep on increasing your precisions, that is reducing the margin of error, and confidence interval from 95% to 99% the sample size increases. E.g., the sample size is 381 for population lavel size of 50,000 at 5% margin of error & at 95%. Confidence, where as for same population at same margin of error but at 99% confidence level, the sample size is 655.

Table. 3.2: Change in Sample Size and Its Selection

Population size	Confidence = 95% Margin of Error				Confidence = 99% Margin of Error			
	5.0%	3.5%	2.5%	1.0%	5.0%	3.5%	2.5%	1.0%
50,000	381	771	1491	8056	655	1318	2520	12455
75,000	382	776	1506	8514	658	1330	2563	13583
100,000	383	778	1513	8762	659	1336	2585	14227
250,000	384	782	1527	9248	662	1347	2626	15555
500,000	384	783	1532	9423	663	1350	2640	16055

Source: https://www.research-advisors.com/tools/SampleSize.htm

In other words, we can say that the results produced with the higher sample size have a better chance of predicting the population. But it will become a tough task to collect the large samples, especially for BBA students as the time frame is short. However, there is a concept of sampling error which can help us in this context. If the **sampling error** is small, we can take small samples as well.

Sample Size Based on The Number of Items in The Scale

Hinkin (1995, 2005) in his studies concluded that the item to response ratio can be used to predict the sample size. It should range from 1:4 to 1:10. e.g. if you got 50 items to measure your concept the sample size will be between 50*4 = 200 (for 1:4) to 50*10 = 500 (for 1:10 ratio).

Rough Estimate

Creswell (2017) provides a rough estimate of sample size for experimental, correlation and survey-based studies:

- In the case of Experimental study, there should be at least 15 participants in each group.
- In the case of correlation studies approximately 30 participants.
- For a survey-based study approximately 350 participants.

3.8 Cronbach Alpha Test for Reliability (Using Software)

This section is covered in chapter 04 under factor analysis.

Tentative Exam Questions

1. Explain the concept of scaling and measurement in research.
2. Explain different scales of measurement.
3. Explain different scaling techniques for measurement.
4. List out the important points on questionnaire design.
5. Explain the fundamentals of scale evaluation in detail.

6. What is sampling? Explain different sampling methods.
7. Explain the different methods for determining sample size.
8. What is the sample size for a population size of 500,000 at different confidence levels & margin of errors?

4

Data and Method of Analysis (Using Excel and R)

> **Syllabus Unit 4:** *Introduction to the statistical software package, MS-Excel and 'R'. Data and method of Analysis: Analysis of Variance (ANOVA), One way and Two-way, Chi-square test (goodness of fit). Multivariate analysis: Factor Analysis (principal component analysis), Discriminant analysis.*

4.1 Introduction to Excel and R for Statistical Data Analysis

Data analysis is one of the main chapters of project or thesis writing as it deals with understanding of our objectives with the help of numbers. There are so many tools in the market for data analysis & presentation, but worldwide MS Excel is used as a beginner's software. Important reasons being, it's easily available, reachable and user-friendly. Among the major contributions of excel to the business world is in the field of calculation and analysis.

To learn excel, lots of resources are there on the internet. However, the preferred is the official Microsoft website for it. Visit **www.support. office.com** (The image below shows the page view of the website and the page view of excel 2016) and look for section '**excel for windows-training**', here lots of resources are waiting for you to learn the basics of excel.

(57)

58 A Concise Handbook of Business Research

Fig. 4.1: Page View of Excel for Windows

Fig. 4.2: Page View of MS-Excel 2016

4.2 Introduction to R

What is 'R'

R is a statistical programming environment which is used worldwide and we personally prefer it over other statistical software like SPSS and Excel. As the previous (SPSS) though very good, is too costly, whereas the later one (the excel), have some limitations which 'R' overcomes comprehensively. So, use R and have fun.

"R is a like a girl of your life whom you love, but she does not talk to you because she does not know you. But, slowly and steadily when the girl starts talking to you, she also starts knowing you, and the picture starts! It is same with R, start talking to it and R will start talking to you and finally one day you will fall in love with it".

R studio: R studio is an upgraded structure of R which is very much user-friendly and is an IDE, that is Integrated Development Environment. It is having GUI i.e. Graphic User interface which makes it more easy to use with added features (For more information log on to https://**cran**.r-project.org, https://www.**rstudio**.com/).

As we will be doing all statistical analysis on R studio so the first step is to download it. Make sure you download first R and then R studio

Downloading 'R'.

Here are the steps

Step 1: Download 'R' from https://cran.r-project.org/

Fig. 4.3: Downloading R

60 A Concise Handbook of Business Research

Step 2: Go to the concerned CRAN mirror as shown in image 2. In the Indian context, you need to download the mirror from https://mirror.niser.ac.in/cran, India.

Fig. 4.4: Downloading R from CRAN Mirror

Step 3: If you are working on windows then click for windows operating system option or else choose according to the appropriate operating system as per your requirement (Linux, Mac etc.). The image is shown below.

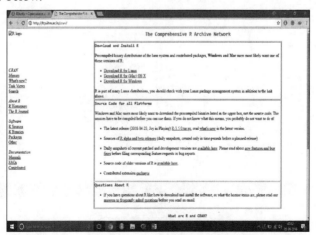

Fig. 4.5: Downloading R for Different Operating System

Data and Method of Analysis   61

R version 3.5.0 is being used in this book for analysis. By the time you may be using it some new version might available (Courtesy – the pandemic due to which the book got delayed). Download this version to practice R.

Step 4: Download R studio from www.rstudio.com and download free R studio desktop option. Click on the windows version as shown through figures (4.6, 4.7, 4.8, 4.9, 4.10).

Fig. 4.6: R Studio Website

Fig. 4.7: Downloading R Studio

62 A Concise Handbook of Business Research

Fig. 4.8: Downloading R Studio Free Version

Fig. 4.9: Downloading R Studio for Different Operating System

Data and Method of Analysis 63

Fig. 4.10: Downloading R Studio Free Version File

Understanding R studio interface.

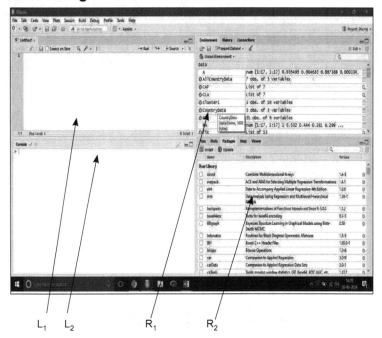

L₁ L₂   R₁   R₂

Fig. 4.11: R studio Interface

When you will open R studio for the first time, you will see four windows (Fig. 4.11).

Let us divide the R studio interface into four windows: L_1, R_1, L_2, and R_2. The upper left-hand corner or L_1 is generally used for writing your scripts or codes for whatever operation you want to run. Whereas the lower window L_2 is called the console. All the commands we write on the L_1 is executed on L_2. All output is generated on L_2.

The R_1 upper window shows us the history of commands we executed in past. If you click on the Environment option in R_1 window, it will show all the dataset and objects used in past. The lower R_2 contain options: Files and Plots (all R files and folder on your computer), Packages (all packages available for different operations which you have to use in your study). It also contains a help section for help related information (see fig. 4.12). If you type for e.g. t.test with a question mark. It will tell R that you are asking for help for this command.

>? t.test

It will show you the syntax for applying the t-test command in R.

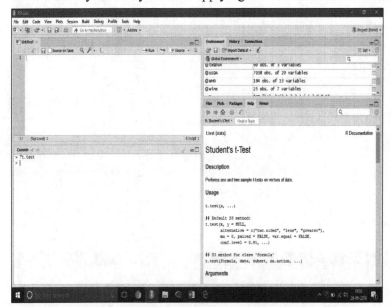

Fig. 4.12: Using Help Section in R Studio

Now check for barplot (A barplot is used to show frequencies, e.g., number of people in different age group) help using the following command.

> ?barplot

This was just a basic introduction of R studio interface. To learn more, we recommend you following links mentioned below. These links are useful learnings on R from top websites, most of them are free. If you do not find a source to be free, go to www.youtube.com. Here you will get a good number of resources on learning R language and statistics.

https://www.rstudio.com/

https://www.datacamp.com/

https://www.analyticsvidhya.com/

https://in.udacity.com/

https://www.udacity.com/

https://www.udemy.com/

https://www.r-bloggers.com/

https://www.edx.org/course/

You need to practice R to use it better. However, we have tried hard to provide you with some key write-ups on methods so that you can understand them and practice them.

Let us also try some hand on experience using R.

Open R studio and type on L_1

2 + 4

Select it (as if you select a word to edit it) and hit run command visible on the top corner of L_1.

If you can make out. You typed a command in a script in L_1 and the output got produced in the console L_2 (Fig. 4.13).

Now type # **I love you**

In your script file L_1.

Select it and hit enter. What happens?

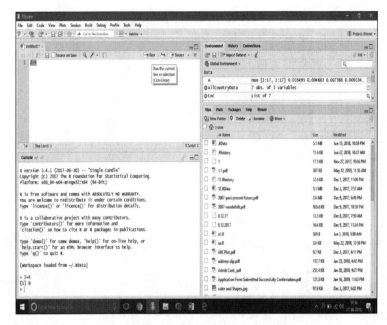

Fig. 4.13: Typing Commands in R Studio

The whole command you typed in the script file comes as it is in the console. The R program read the commands with '#' signs as an instruction for our self-use and not for any operation. So, use # command whenever you want to remind things for self.

Now we leave you here for practice the basics of R using the mentioned links and let us continue with the syllabus. Without practicing the basics of R it will be really tough, so make sure you invest at least 10-30 days basic workout and then move to the statistical analysis portion.

4.3 Data and Method of Analysis

This chapter is about performing statistical operations and testing your assumptions (Hypothesis). Let us start by understanding the term data analysis and the methods of analysis.

'Data analysis' is about generating meaning from the data which you have collected through primary and secondary data sources e.g. the

Data and Method of Analysis   67

primary data collected through your questionnaire or the secondary data of balance sheets of companies which you have collected from websites like www.moneycontrol.com.

Here methods of data analysis mean different statistical approaches and tools to examine data. More the variables are in your study (e.g. public-sector banks, private sector banks, employee age, gender) and the importance of the relationship between variables, the tools used to analyze the data changes and become more rigorous. These methods come under quantitative methods. So, you should learn your statistics subject well to implement quantitative tools. However, we have tried our best to make you understand the concepts with the least mathematical calculations. To make this possible we have taken the help of computer-based software like **MS-Excel and 'R'**. Will discuss more about them as the chapter goes on. Let us first summarize important data analysis tools based on the syllabus we are following. We can put them into four categories on the basis of the level of complexities of use and on the number of variables for analysis:

1. Data visualization using graphs, Descriptive Analysis

2. Bivariate Analysis: Correlation, Regression, t-test, ANOVA and Chi-square test.

3. Multivariate Analysis: Multiple Regression, MANOVA, and

4. Classifying and grouping data analysis: Discriminant Analysis, Conjoint Analysis, Factor Analysis, and Cluster Analysis.

Category one is level one analysis of our data. Data visualization helps us in finding the pattern, shape and size of the data using graphs & charts whereas, the descriptive analysis performs the same but more descriptively using expressing parameters like mean, variance, skewness, maximum value, minimum value etc as numbers. It is mostly used for single variable analysis. When dealing with two variables analysis, we use the second category (Bivariate analysis) and when dealing with three or more variables analysis we use the third category (Multivariate analysis). We have created one more category fourth, the classifying and grouping data analysis. They also come under multivariate analysis but their use is in classifying and grouping data, e.g. creating market segments (Discriminant analysis), grouping customer preferences (conjoint analysis used for market research), creating recommendation system just like in your NETFLIX for other related movies, grouping employees on the basis of performance (cluster analysis), grouping variables under a common theme so that number of variables can be reduced or justified (factor analysis).

We can also fit these four categories into two broad statistics categorizations. One is Descriptive statistics (category 1) and another inferential statistic (category 2, 3 or 4). The objective of descriptive statistics is to describe the data: Its shape, size, and pattern. The objective of inferential statistics is to predict the behavior and validate assumptions about a population from a sample (because the population is too big). now let us see these categorization in detail.

4.3.1 Data Visualization

To understand the pattern in the data the first and the foremost method to be used by a business research student is to visualize the data using graphs and figures e.g. Like bar chart or pie chart. The basic idea behind using them is to sense the data. Let us visualize a graph below and try to find what information we can extract from our data using graphs and diagrams.

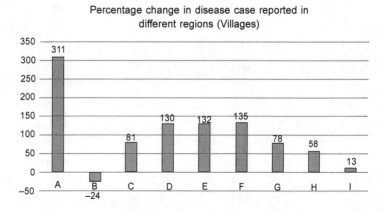

Fig. 4.14: BAR Chart

Data and Method of Analysis 69

This is a BAR chart visualizing the percentage change in diseases case reported in different regions (A, B, C, D, E, F, G, H, I). From the bar graph (fig. 4.14), it is very much clear that the village 'A' showed 311% increase in disease reported whereas the village 'B' showed a 24% decrease in disease cases reported.

What else can you visualize in this graph? Do tell your class teacher in the discussion.

For more data visualization exercises go to https://trends.google.com/trend/ and start visualizing the data, e.g. search your college name and see how many times it has been viewed internationally and then compared it with my Gurukula Kangri Vishwavidyalaya.

Just to show you, we did a comparison of our university with IIT Roorkee (Fig. 4.15). The line graph shows the trend for the last year of both the institution on the basis of how many times the keywords have been hit.

"Visit this website and start comparing the things you want. Have fun!"

Fig. 4.15: Data Visualization Exercise Using https://trends.google.com/trends/

Descriptive Analysis

Descriptive analysis (also known as summary statistics) is a summary of key statistics which helps in understanding data using numbers. It is more concerned with the values of Mean, Standard Error, Median, Mode, Standard, Deviation, Sample Variance, Kurtosis, Skewness, Range, Minimum, Maximum, Sum, and Counts. Learn your statistics subject well to understand these terms better.

Descriptive Analysis using Excel

For performing data analysis in Excel first you need to install the data analysis pack. The procedure is:

Step 1: Open MS-Excel spreadsheet.

Step 2: Go to file in the menu, then click it, then go to options menu, click it and then to add inns.

(*for 2007 excel version click the Microsoft Office button and then click options)

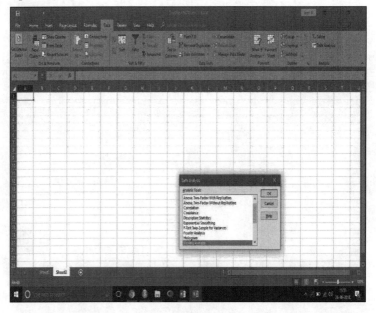

Fig. 4.16: Downloading Data Analysis Pack in MS Excel

Data and Method of Analysis 71

Step 3: After Add inns, a window opens up, click on Analysis Tool Pack, then click 'Go' and then ok. The data analysis pack will get installed in your computer MS-Excel.

(*If Analysis ToolPak is not listed in the Add-Ins available box, click Browse to locate it. If you are prompted that the Analysis ToolPak is not currently installed on your computer, click Yes to install it.)

Step 4: Now then go to Data on the forehead of your excel sheet, click it see at the rightmost corner Data Analysis might be visible to you, click on it (fig. 4.16).

Step 5: Then choose the required statistical tool.

Explaining Data Analysis using Descriptive Statistics

Let us take an example of a filled-in questionnaire and try to figure it out what is the descriptive statistics outcome we can make using excel. This is a snapshot of a questionnaire used by my one of the students (Table 4.1).

Table: 4.1: A sample Questionnaire for Descriptive Analysis

Respondent	CA/ITL	Experience	Age	Q.1	Q.2	Q.3
1	CA	1-5yr	30-40	Agree	Neutral	Strongly Agree
2	ITL	20-25yr	40-50	Strongly Agree	Strongly Agree	Strongly Agree
3	ITL	5-10yr	30-40	Agree	Neutral	Strongly Agree
4	ITL	10-15yr	40-50	Agree	Agree	Strongly Agree
5	ITL	15-20yr	40-50	Disagree	Disagree	Strongly Disagree
6	CA	1-5yr	30-40	Strongly Agree	Agree	Agree
7	CA	10-15yr	40-50	Agree	Neutral	Strongly Agree
8	CA	5-10yr	30-40	Strongly Agree	Agree	Agree
9	ITL	10-15yr	40-50	Strongly Agree	Neutral	Agree

Contd.../Table 4.1

72 A Concise Handbook of Business Research

Respondent	CA/ITL	Experience	Age	Q.1	Q.2	Q.3
10	ITL	15-20yr	50-60	Strongly Agree	Strongly Agree	Strongly Agree
11	ITL	15-20yr	40-50	Agree	Strongly Agree	Strongly Agree
12	ITL	10-15yr	40-50	Strongly Disagree	Disagree	agree
13	ITL	15-20yr	50-60	Strongly Disagree	Neutral	Strongly Agree
14	ITL	5-10yr	30-40	Strongly Disagree	Neutral	Strongly Agree
15	ITL	10-15yr	30-40	Strongly Agree	Agree	Strongly Disagree
16	ITL	10-15yr	40-50	Strongly Agree	Agree	Strongly Disagree
17	ITL	15-20yr	40-50	Strongly Agree	Agree	Agree
18	CA	5-10yr	30-40	Strongly Agree	Strongly Agree	Strongly Agree

CA = Charted Accountant and ITL = Income Tax lawyer
Strongly Disagree = 1   Disagree = 2   Neutral = 3   Agree = 4   Strongly Agree = 5 (here also)

Now for data analysis we need to convert same non-numeric data to numeric data. So convert Q-1 to Q-3 according to the details above.

The descriptive statistics Q-1 to Q-3 in Excel using a descriptive analysis package will give you the following results (Table 4.2).

Table 4.2: Descriptive Statistics Output in Excel 2016

Column 1		Column 2		Column 3	
Mean	2.29	Mean	1.82	Mean	2.53
Standard Error	0.35	Standard Error	0.36	Standard Error	0.37
Median	2.00	Median	2.00	Median	2.00
Mode	2.00	Mode	0.00	Mode	2.00
Standard Deviation	1.45	Standard Deviation	1.47	Standard Deviation	1.55
Sample Variance	2.10	Sample Variance	2.15	Sample Variance	2.39
Kurtosis	-0.68	Kurtosis	-1.32	Kurtosis	-0.76
Skewness	0.12	Skewness	0.21	Skewness	0.00
Range	5.00	Range	4.00	Range	5.00

Contd.../Table 4.2

Column 1		Column 2		Column 3	
Minimum	0.00	Minimum	0.00	Minimum	0.00
Maximum	5.00	Maximum	4.00	Maximum	5.00
Sum	39.00	Sum	31.00	Sum	43.00
Count	17.00	Count	17.00	Count	17.00

For more details on mean, median, mode etc. contact your statistics teacher.

However, for the data in a category in the data sheet above like that of a number of respondents and their classification, their experience, you can use the Pivot table function in excel. Again, go to the top menu bar in the excel sheet, go to the '**insert**' section and click '**Pivot table**'. After clicking it, a new window opens up (generally on the lower side of the screen) which asks 'choose the data you want to analyze', then select the data set range you want to analyze. Select all data set and hit ok. A big new window 'Pivot Table Fields' will pop up on the right side of the excel sheet. Choose those variables which you want to analyze and drag them to section "drag fields between the area below", e.g. If you want to analyze the distribution of total 18 respondents according to their profession (CA/Income Tax Lawyer) and age group, then drag CA/ITL in row and age to two sections, column and values section. You will see a table like this (fig. 4.17).

Count of Age	Column Label ▾			
Row Label ▾	30-40	40-50	50-60	Grand Total
CA	4	1		5
ITL	3	8	2	13
Grand Total	7	9	2	18

Fig. 4.17: Output of Pivot Table in MS-Excel

From this table we can see that out of total 18 respondents, 7 belongs to the 30-40 age group, 9 belongs to the 40-50 age group and 02 belongs to the 50-60 age group. Overall there are 05 CA's and 13 Income tax lawyers. Go for more options using the above data sheet.

Descriptive Analysis Using Software 'R'

From here throughout this book, 'R' means 'R' studio as all analysis is done on R studio.

First, open R studio window. On the top ribbon, some icons are there, click on 'view' and click on the 'panes' section, in it click 'all panes' section. Hope all windows to work on gets open. Now you need to install a readxl package which is used to read excel files. So, the first type in your console

>install. Packages ("readxl")

Two, go to the 'file menu', then to 'import dataset' and click on 'excel' your excel file will be loaded.

Type the command **str ()** to get the structure of your dataset

Type the command **summary ()** to get the descriptive statistics.

Let us start doing an example in R

I will first read a file 'gst.xls' stored in my D drive and will perform operations (Fig. 4.18).

Fig. 4.18: Importing Excel File in R Studio

Let's us do it in R console (**remember we are typing it directly in the R console because we remember commands. You should type all**

Data and Method of Analysis   75

your commands in the L1 window (as you can save them) and read the output in L2 window).

After loading the dataset, your screen on R studio will show this (Fig. 4.19).

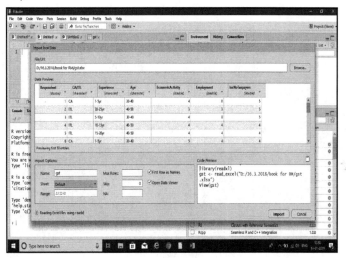

Fig. 4.19: Importing Excel File in R (Page View)

Then click Import, the excel sheet will be ready for operations (Fig. 4.20).

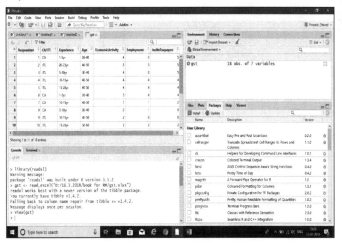

Fig. 4.20: Imported Excel File in R Studio-1

76 A Concise Handbook of Business Research

Now type command:

> **str(gst)**

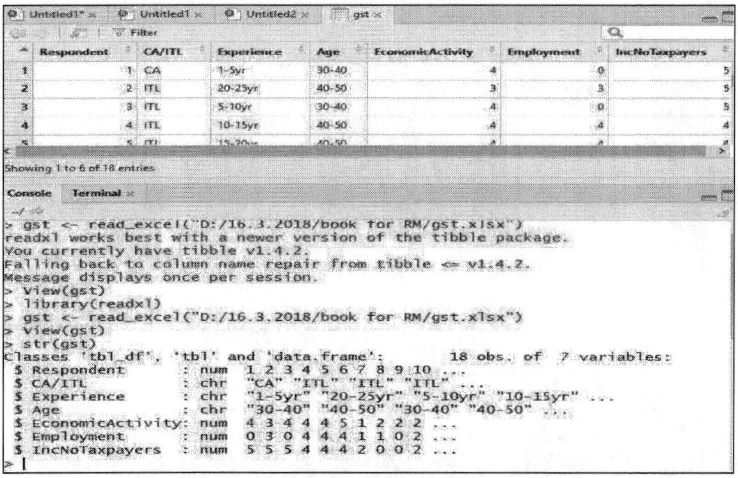

Fig. 4.21: Imported Excel file in R Studio-2

Here now what we are showing you is the left-hand side of the screen for the better view, the L1 and L2 (Fig. 4.21).

Now type **summary(gst)** to get descriptive statistics (Fig. 4.22).

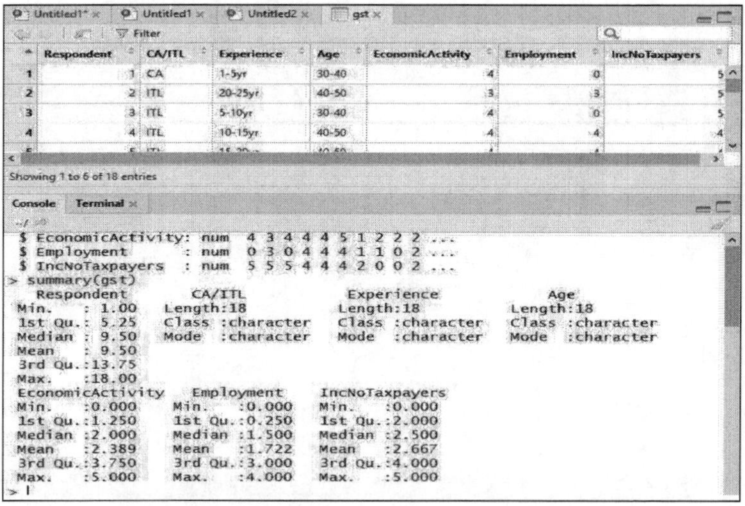

Fig. 4.22: Descriptive Statistics Output in R Studios

By this, you will get your descriptive statistics, discuss with your class teacher the statistical summary.

Here we encountered one problem, that is the variables: CA/ITL, Experience, and Age were shown as a character on which it is hard to produce statistical operations. For that, we need to convert them into factors. So, make sure the variables for calculation should either be numeric or factors.

We have to perform the following commands so that we can work on data.

By the first three commands, we converted the character variables into factor variables so that statistical operations can be used (Fig. 4.23). Do visualize the descriptive statistics and discuss that with your class teacher.

> gst$`CA/ITL`=factor(gst$`CA/ITL`)

> gst$Experience=factor(gst$Experience)

> gst$Age=factor(gst$Age)

> summary(gst)

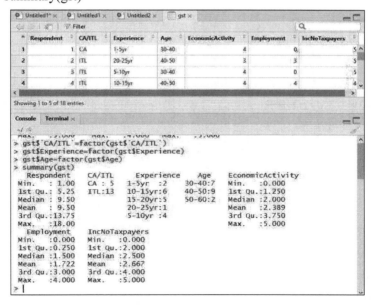

Fig. 4.23: Converting Characters to Variables for Data Analysis in R

78 A Concise Handbook of Business Research

Can you make out the difference between characters, numeric and factor variables seeing the two above slides?

Here the descriptive statistic output is produced by R. Discuss all these points with your class teacher.

4.3.2 Bivariate Analysis

Bivariate analysis means we are talking about two variables analysis. E.g. advertisement impact on sales.

Analysis of Variance (ANOVA)

What is ANOVA?

Analysis of variance, also called as ANOVA, is a collection of methods used for comparing multiple means across different groups (Khan Academy, n.d.).It is also an important method under experimental design where we are interested in measuring the difference between three or more groups.

Two variations are of consideration when we calculate ANOVA, the variance which exists between the samples (e.g. the difference which may exist between two class sections say section A and Section B, on the average marks scored. This variance is attributed to sample means) and, the variance which exist within the samples (which may be attributed to sampling). Comparing these two kinds of variances is key to ANOVA analysis.

F Ratio: The ratio of two variances i.e. between group variance and within group variance is called the F ratio. The higher it is the better it is. The F ratio value if comes out to be significant at a set p-value (visible in your data output window) means that your groups are significantly different. Or understand like this if the output window shows that the p-value is below .01/.05/.10 set level. We say that the F ratio is significant and the groups are different.

Data and Method of Analysis 79

Following Assumptions are to be taken care of when using ANOVA in the calculation (Bajpai, 2011).

- The samples should belong to a normally distributed population (Read normal distribution in detail)
- The process of sample selection is random.
- The samples drawn are independent of each other.
- The populations should have equal variance.

When to use?

ANOVA methods come handy under experimental method and quasi-experimental methods where you are trying to measure the impact of a variable on a population. This is performed by conducting an experiment in which you choose samples and check to what extent the variable is affecting the samples. Here the 'variable' we are talking about is the independent variable, whereas the 'samples' is the dependent variable.

ANOVA is used when we need to study more than two populations. Generally, we use a t-test for comparing means when we have two populations but when the number of the population under study exceeds two, we use ANOVA.

You may also be interested in finding what impact is visible as the interaction between the variables, in this case also ANOVA comes in handy (See two-way ANOVA example further to understand interaction effect).

As the name suggests the ANOVA test measures the difference between the group on the basis of variances in the samples both within the sample and between the sample. It tries to capture not only the means difference but also the variances exist inside it.

The F ratio is the ratio which takes the ratio of these two variances as mentioned above.

Let me make it clearer. Take a case where you are interested in finding the difference between three class sections on the basis of marks attained

80 A Concise Handbook of Business Research

by them in the subject say statistics. In this case, ANOVA analysis can tell you whether the groups differ significantly from each other or not on the basis of marks attained and here you cannot use independent sample t-test because it is having more than two variables'

Let us take another example where you might be interested in measuring the impact of three different books, say A, B, C used in three different class sections I, II, III to measure their impact on their marks. Here we can also visualize whether the class section and Book together have some impact on marks (interaction effect) or is it because of the variables individually.

The first example discussed (e.g. of statistic subject) is a case of One-Way ANOVA and the second example discussed (e.g. of book in classes above) is an example of Two -Way ANOVA.

In One-way ANOVA you are interested in comparing the means of two or more groups (dependent variables) with respect to a single categorical factor (independent variable). Let us take another example, if you are interested in finding the impact of Disprin tablet and paracetamol (independent variables) on a headache (Dependent variable), then we are talking about one-way ANOVA. In this, treatment is a between-group factor with one levels, i.e., type of medicines.

However, if we add one more variable (more in terms of factor or category) to it like say the time frame i.e. we may see the impact of the medicines over the period of time say 6 months and 01 years, it becomes a Two-way ANOVA case., because here we may be interested in finding the impact of medicines on headache for respondents over two different time frames.

This type of design contains both within group design w.r.t to the timeframe and between-group design w.r.t to two medicines impact on a headache.

When we go only with a time frame for the same sample. It is called a *repeated measure design*. Because here the sample does not change. e.g. if we check the long-term impact of dispersion for two different time period is an example of it.

Crossing two or more factors produces Two-way ANOVA, similarly, for three factors, it is three-way ANOVA and so on.

Here in two-way ANOVA, three F ratios will be seen. One for between medicines, one for time and one for the interaction of medicines over time.

If the test of significance shows that the F ratios are significant i.e. their p-value is less the set significance level (.05, .01 or .10) we say that the difference is significant between group/within group/or interaction effect.

How to use (One-Way ANOVA)?

Q1. Veera Shoes Ltd. is a leading manufacturer of shoes in Uttarakhand. The company has launched its new design in the four main cities of Uttarakhand: Dehradun, Haridwar, Nainital, US Nagar. The company told the retailers and its customers that the brand would be sold out at a uniform price throughout the state. However, the company got the feedback from the market that the retailers are selling its new design at a different price which can affect the image of the company. To get into the matter the company collected data on price fluctuation across cities on its product. It randomly collected information on six samples (price per pair of shoes of new design) from each city.

Price for the pair of shoes (in Rupees)

Dehradun	Haridwar	Nainital	US Nagar
1900	1800	2100	2200
1900.50	1700	2000	2200.50
1900	1800.50	2100.50	2100.50
2000	1700	2000	2200
1900	1800.50	2100	2200.50
2100	1700	2000	2100.50

But, before moving on to the excel sheet let us see a few steps needed by a researcher to reach on any conclusion.

Solution: In this journey of Research Methodology (RM), it is being told you that RM is a systematic field of inquiry, and among the steps one key step is hypothesis testing (see chapter one), i.e. testing our set

82 A Concise Handbook of Business Research

assumptions in a systematic way. Here the assumption is that the price of shoes might be fluctuating between cities.

To test this assumption and to get to a conclusion we follow certain steps.

Step 1. Set the null and alternate hypothesis

Null hypothesis: a standard hypothesis where we claim that there exists no difference between the variables. Represented by Ho.

In our example, in this hypothesis, we claim that the prices of shoes in all four cities are equal or there is no difference in the prices of this design in four cities.

Alternative Hypothesis: A hypothesis or assumption which we want to prove should come takes place in an alternative hypothesis. For example, in our case, the difference in the prices we think might be there will go into this alternative hypothesis part. It is represented by H1.

Step 2. Determine the appropriate statistical test.

For comparing means we have t-test (One variable and two variables), ANOVA (more than two variables)

For measuring association, we have a correlation.

For measuring dependence and overall model fit: we have Regression Analysis, Chi-square test (for categorical data), Structured Equation Modelling (combination of Confirmatory Factor Analysis (CFA) and Regression Analysis).

For reducing dimensions in the questionnaire, we have Principle Component Analysis (Example reducing the number of variables to few such that the maximum impact is visible by those few variables).

For creating factors from a small number of variables we have Factor Analysis. When we want to explore about how many factors we should have or when we are trying to create factors from many small numbers of variables, we are talking about Exploratory Factor Analysis and when we want to test a model with confirmed factors, we are talking about Confirmatory Factor Analysis (CFA). For classification problems we have: Cluster Analysis

Data and Method of Analysis 83

This is not an exhaustive list it is a broad list of major tests which you may require in your study depending on the type of data, complexity of the problem and relationship among variables (Also read the difference between parametric & non-parametric tests).

Step 3: Set the significance level and the decision rule (α-alpha and p-value concept)

The level of significance denotes the probability of rejecting the null hypothesis when it is true. Denoted by 'α'.

The values of 'α' for research purpose taken are: .05, .01, and .10 (least priority)

Here .05 means that the researcher is 95% confident that the right decision has been made (there is only 5 chance of out of 100 that the null hypothesis will be rejected).

This region of 95% is the critical region under the normal curve.

'P' value concept for accepting and rejecting the null hypothesis in statistical software: In the p-value approach neither a significance level nor a critical value is determined before the experiment is carried out or the sample taken. The null and alternative hypotheses are stated, and the experiment is run. A statistics is computed from the outcome of the experiment

The p-value is the probability of observing a sample value as extreme as, or more extreme than, the value actually observed, given that the null hypothesis is true. This area represents the probability of a Type I error that must be assumed if the null hypothesis is rejected. The p-value is compared to the significance level.

If the p-value is less than the significance level, the null hypothesis is rejected (if p-value $< \alpha$, reject the null). If p is greater than or equal to the significance level, the null hypothesis is not rejected (if p-value $> \alpha$, don't reject the null).

It is the second method of presenting the results of a statistical test, which reports the extent to which the test statistic disagrees with the null hypothesis. This method has become popular because analysts want to know what percentage of the sampling distribution lies beyond the sample statistic on the curve, and most statistical computer programs report the results of statistical tests as probability values (p values).

Step 4: Collect the sample data

Step 5: Analyze the data by implementing appropriate tests

Step 6: Accepting or rejecting the Null hypothesis and Interpreting its meaning for the business world.

Now let us find out the truth of the price fluctuation. Get set go!!

Doing One-Way ANOVA Using Excel.

Do one thing create this table on excel or copy paste it. Go to the Data Analysis pack and select the ANOVA Single Factor. Then select all the numeric portion of all the three columns as shown in the image below (fig 4.24). Save the output in the new worksheet.

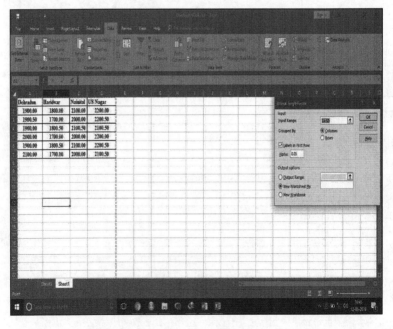

Fig. 4.24: Doing One Way ANOVA in Excel.

Data and Method of Analysis 85

Table 4.3: One Way ANOVA Output in Excel.

Anova: Single Factor						
SUMMARY						
Groups	Count	Sum	Average	Variance		
Dehradun	6.00	11700.50	1950.08	6990.04		
Haridwar	6.00	10501.00	1750.17	3020.07		
Nainital	6.00	12300.50	2050.08	3010.04		
US Nagar	6.00	13002.00	2167.00	2653.40		
ANOVA						
Source of Variation	**SS**	**df**	**MS**	**F**	**P-value**	**F crit**
Between Groups	561583.58	3.00	187194.53	47.77	0.00	3.10
Groups	78367.75	20.00	3918.39			
Total	639951.33	23.00				

Output Summary: From the Excel output (table 4.3) we can say that at 95% confidence interval the F-critical value visible is 3.10 which is the table value of F at .05 confidence level and at 3,20 (between group degree of freedom, within group degree of freedom) if you see the F table in any of statistics book. The calculated value of F is 47.77 (simply written F in excel table) which is clearly greater than the tabular value (F-crit. in the table above) of 3.10.

Hence the null hypothesis i.e. the set assumption that there is no difference between the different cities on shoe pair prices are clearly rejected as the p-value is 0.00 which is below the set significance level of .05. Hence, we accept the alternative hypothesis and will say that "there is a significant difference between the prices in different cities".

So, the Veera shoes Ltd should tighten the screws of the retailers and should warn them of making the uniformity across cities.

One-Way ANOVA using R

But for this, we have to make a certain change in the excel table (As Shown in Table 4.4). Because ANOVA is the type of generalized linear model it understands the language of the independent and dependent variable in R. Here as far as our problem is concerned, we have two variables four cities and their respective prices. Here cities are independent variable and price is a dependent variable. Arrange the variables only in two columns for R calculations. Here we have arranged in four columns due to limited space.

Table 4.4: Modifying Excel Table for Calculating One Way ANOVA in R.

Cities	Price	Cities	Price
DD	1900.00	NAIN	2100.00
DD	1900.50	NAIN	2000.00
DD	1900.00	NAIN	2100.50
DD	2000.00	NAIN	2000.00
DD	1900.00	NAIN	2100.00
DD	2100.00	NAIN	2000.00
HDR	1800.00	USN	2200.00
HDR	1700.00	USN	2200.50
HDR	1800.50	USN	2100.50
HDR	1700.00	USN	2200.00
HDR	1800.50	USN	2200.50
HDR	1700.00	USN	2100.50

Here DD = Dehradun, HDR = Haridwar, NAIN = Nainital, USN = US Nagar.

Here cities will be treated as factors and price as continuous data.

Click on Import and your file is ready to use (fig 4.25). We have saved this file in excel format by name 'one-way ANOVA'.

Now first use the basic two commands to get a feel for your data.

>str (one-way ANOVA)

Here we find that the data set if having the cities variable as a numeric variable. Let us convert that into factors for ANOVA calculation.

Data and Method of Analysis 87

Fig. 4.25: Doing One Way ANOVA in R.

>OneWayANOVA$Cities= factor (OneWayANOVA$Cities)
>str (one-way ANOVA)
> summary (one-way ANOVA)

Cities	Price
DD: 6	Min. :1700
HRD :6	1st Qu.:1875
NAIN:6	Median :2000
USN :6	Mean :1979
3rd Qu.:2100	
Max. :2200	

> fit < – aov(Price~Cities, data = OneWayANOVA)

> summary(fit)

	Df	Sum Sq	Mean Sq	F value	Pr(>F)
Cities	3	561584	187195	47.77	2.65e-09 ***
Residuals	20	78368	3918		

Signif. codes: 0 '***' 0.001 '**' 0.01 '*' 0.05 '.' 0.1 ' ' 1

88 A Concise Handbook of Business Research

Fig. 4.26: One Way ANOVA Output in R.

As shown in fig. 4.26, we have used 'aov' command to perform ANOVA analysis. Then we have saved its output in a variable name 'fit'. But at this moment the R will not show you output and here then you have to use summary(fit) to reflect the R output.

The output shows that the prices of four cities are significantly different at 0.001 which is way below the set decision rule of .05 earlier. The P r(>F) value 2.65e-09 shows that this value is very very small! It is 0.0000000265 which if you round out to two digits is 0.00 actually so don't be confused with the p values using 'e' sign.

So, in summary, city prices are significantly different.

Try to compare the output of R and Excel and discuss with your friends & class teachers..

A Problem on Two-Way ANOVA

For performing two-way ANOVA let us take a dataset from a good source on the internet.

Day	News	Business	Sports
Monday	11	10	4
	8	12	3
	6	13	5

Contd...

Data and Method of Analysis 89

Day	News	Business	Sports
	8	11	6
Tuesday	9	7	5
	10	8	8
	10	11	6
	12	9	7
Wednesday	8	7	5
	9	8	9
	9	10	7
	11	9	6
Thursday	4	9	7
	5	6	6
	3	8	6
	5	8	5
Friday	13	10	12
	12	9	10
	11	9	11
	14	8	12

Source: (http://college.cengage.com/mathematics/brase/understandable_
statistics/7e/students/datasets/twan/frames/frame.html)

The dataset is about advertisement in local newspapers and the response generated by them. The details are:

- Response: Number of inquiries resulting from advertisement.
- Factor 1: Day of week (Monday through Friday)
- Factor 2: Section of newspaper (News, Business, Sports)
- Here we are interested in three of the following:

Is there any significant difference in responses when we consider days?

Ho = There is no significant difference in responses when we consider days in a week.

Is there any significant difference in responses when we consider the Newspaper section?

Ho = There is no significant difference in responses when we consider three newspaper sections.

Is there any interaction effect of the newspaper section with days for responses?

Ho = There is no significant difference between responses even if we take the interaction of newspaper section and weekdays.

Two Way ANOVA using Excel

Open excel file go to data analysis pack click on Two factor ANOVA with replication. Here we used Two Factor with Replication because we have more than one column category. Else we have used ANOVA without replication. Select the data set as usual but here excel will ask for one option i.e. a number of rows per factor (fig. 4.27). In our case, there are four samples each day.

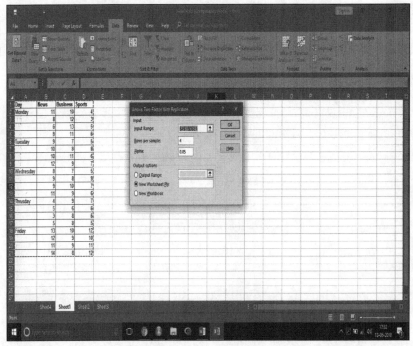

Fig. 4.27: Doing Two Way ANOVA in Excel

Data and Method of Analysis 91

Table 4.5: Two-Way ANOVA Output in Excel

ANOVA: Two-Factor with Replication						
SUMMARY	News	Business	Sports	Total		
Monday						
Count	4	4	4	12		
Sum	33	46	18	97		
Average	8.25	11.5	4.5	8.083333		
Variance	4.25	1.666667	1.666667	10.99242		
Tuesday						
Count	4	4	4	12		
Sum	41	35	26	102		
Average	10.25	8.75	6.5	8.5		
Variance	1.583333	2.916667	1.666667	4.272727		
Wednesday						
Count	4	4	4	12		
Sum	37	34	27	98		
Average	9.25	8.5	6.75	8.166667		
Variance	1.583333	1.666667	2.916667	2.878788		
Thursday						
Count	4	4	4	12		
Sum	17	31	24	72		
Average	4.25	7.75	6	6		
Variance	0.916667	1.583333	0.666667	3.090909		
Friday						
Count	4	4	4	12		
Sum	50	36	45	131		
Average	12.5	9	11.25	10.91667		
Variance	1.666667	0.666667	0.916667	3.174242		
Total						
Count	20	20	20			
Sum	178	182	140			
Average	8.9	9.1	7			
Variance	9.357895	3.042105	6.631579			
ANOVA						
Source of Variation	SS	df	MS	F	P-value	F crit

Contd...

92 A Concise Handbook of Business Research

ANOVA: Two-Factor with Replication						
SUMMARY	News	Business	Sports	Total		
Sample	146.8333	4	36.70833	20.90981	8.52E-10	2.578739
Columns	53.73333	2	26.86667	15.3038	8.5E-06	3.204317
Interaction	135.7667	8	16.97083	9.66693	1.12E-07	2.152133
Within	79	45	1.755556			
Total	415.3333	59				

Form the Excel output (table 4.5), in short, we can summarize that there is a significant difference in responses to the advertisement when compared to three sections (p-value = 8.52E-10): News, Business, Sports. There is a significant difference in responses when compared to five days (p-value =.8.5E-06). There is also a significant difference in the responses when we take the interaction effect of days with newspaper section(p=1.12E-07).

Hence, we reject all the null hypothesis and accept the alternate hypothesis in this case.

(**Note** = Hope you are not confused with the p-value in this form '**8.52E-10**'. It means that this value is very very small! and is equal to **0.000000000085**2. For sake of understanding, you can round the digits to last three digits in excel. It will now look 0.000 after rounding off.)

Two-Way ANOVA using R

Now let us do the same problem using R. Here, first we need to rearrange the excel sheet to get the dependent and independent variables clearly visible (table 4.6). As told before Anova is a special case of linear models just like your regression analysis. The arranged table will look like this.

Table 4.6: Modifying Excel Table for Calculating Two-Way ANOVA in R.

Day	News Section	Responses
Monday	News	11
Monday	News	8
Monday	News	6
Monday	News	8

Contd.../Table 4.6

Data and Method of Analysis 93

Day	News Section	Responses
Tuesday	News	9
Tuesday	News	10
Tuesday	News	10
Tuesday	News	12
Wednesday	News	8
Wednesday	News	9
Wednesday	News	9
Wednesday	News	11
Thursday	News	4
Thursday	News	5
Thursday	News	3
Thursday	News	5
Friday	News	13
Friday	News	12
Friday	News	11
Friday	News	14
Monday	Business	10
Monday	Business	12
Monday	Business	13
Monday	Business	11
Tuesday	Business	7
Tuesday	Business	8
Tuesday	Business	11
Tuesday	Business	9
Wednesday	Business	7
Wednesday	Business	8
Wednesday	Business	10
Wednesday	Business	9
Thursday	Business	9
Thursday	Business	6
Thursday	Business	8
Thursday	Business	8
Friday	Business	10
Friday	Business	9

Contd.../Table 4.6

94 A Concise Handbook of Business Research

Day	News Section	Responses
Friday	Business	9
Friday	Business	8
Monday	Sports	4
Monday	Sports	3
Monday	Sports	5
Monday	Sports	6
Tuesday	Sports	5
Tuesday	Sports	8
Tuesday	Sports	6
Tuesday	Sports	7
Wednesday	Sports	5
Wednesday	Sports	9
Wednesday	Sports	7
Wednesday	Sports	6
Thursday	Sports	7
Thursday	Sports	6
Thursday	Sports	6
Thursday	Sports	5
Friday	Sports	12
Friday	Sports	10
Friday	Sports	11
Friday	Sports	12

Now lets us load the data set in R same as before we did for other files.

> library(readxl)

> twan04 <- read_excel("C:/Users/Ashish/Downloads/twan04.xls")

> View(twan04)

> str(twan04)

Classes 'tbl_df', 'tbl' and 'data.frame': 60 obs. of 3 variables:

$ Day : chr "Monday" "Monday" "Monday" "Monday" ...

$ NewsSection: chr "News" "News" "News" "News" ...

$ Responses : num 11 8 6 8 9 10 10 12 8 9 ...

Data and Method of Analysis   95

Here we can see that the two factors in our model are still in character mode so first, we need to convert them into factors from characters

Using the following operation we will get what we want.

> twan04$Day=factor(twan04$Day)

> twan04$NewsSection=factor(twan04$NewsSection)

Checking again using str () command we will structure of our data frame.

> str(twan04)

Classes 'tbl_df', 'tbl' and 'data.frame':
60 obs. of 3 variables:

$ Day : Factor w/ 5 levels "Friday", "Monday",..: 2 2 2 2 4 4 4 4 5 5 ...

$ NewsSection: Factor w/ 3 levels "Business","News",..: 2 2 2 2 2 2 2 2 2 2 ...

$ Responses : num 11 8 6 8 9 10 10 12 8 9 ...

Here we can clearly identify that we are talking about two factors One is Newspaper section and the other is the week day. That's why we are using two way Anova.

```
> summary(twan04)
            Day            NewsSectionso        Responses
Friday   :  12          Business : 20        Min.   :  3.000
Monday   :  12          News     : 20        1st Qu. :  6.000
Thursday :  12          Sports   : 20        Median :  8.000
Tuesday  :  12          Mean     : 8.333     3rd Qu. : 10.000
Wednesday:  12                               Max.     : 14.000
> fit<-aov (Responses~Day*NewsSection, data=twan04)
> summary(fit)
```

	Df	Sum Sq	Mean Sq	F value	Pr(>F)
Day	4	146.83	36.71	20.910	8.52e-10 ***
NewsSection	2	53.73	26.87	15.304	8.50e-06 ***
Day:NewsSection	8	135.77	16.97	9.667	1.12e-07 ***
Residuals	45	79.00	1.76		

Signif. codes: 0 '***' 0.001 '**' 0.01 '*' 0.05 '.' 0.1 ' ' 1

Interpreting the R output for Two-way ANOVA

From the summary table, we can see that p-value ie Pr(>F) is having three stars. Which means the p values are significant for Day, NewsSection and the interaction of Day and News Section (also see Fig. 4.28).

What does significance mean here?

Here significance means that the responses of advertisement are affected by the day chosen for advertisement; by News Section of advertisement and also the combination of day and news section.

Hence rejecting the null hypothesis and accepting alternative hypothesis that is there is a significant difference in responses in the two factors and even on the basis of the day and news section interaction.

Fig. 4.28: Two-Way ANOVA Output in R

You might be interested in visualizing the effect of these factors on responses (see fig. 4.29).

So, install a few packages like "gplots", "HH" for it. Here the effects of factors on responses is shown with the help of HH package.

> install. Packages("HH")

> library(HH)

> interaction2wt (Responses~Day*News Section, data=twan04)

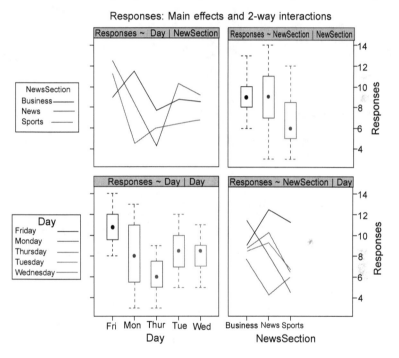

Fig. 4.29: Visualizing Main Effects and Interaction Effect

Let us discuss the interaction effect of Day and News Section on Responses.

- For Friday we can see that the News section has better responses than the Business and Sports section.
- For Monday the Business section has a better response than News and Sports.

98 A Concise Handbook of Business Research

- For Thursday the Business section has a better response than Sports and News.
- For Tuesday the News section has a better response than Business and Sports.
- For Wednesday the News section has a better response than Business and Sports.

So, we can say that there is a great deal of fluctuation in the response in the overall interaction model. For Tuesday, Wednesday and Friday the maximum responses are for an advertisement from the News section. Whereas for Monday and Thursday the maximum responses are from the advertisement in Business Section.

Chi-Square Test

Also called as the goodness of fit test denoted by '$\chi 2$' is a test used to check the relationship between two categorical variables. The test helps us to define whether the dependent variable, actually dependent on the independent variable or not.

When observations are classified on the basis of two variables and arranged in a table, the resulting table is referred to as a contingency table Chi-square test of independence uses this table for determining the independence of two variables). This is why the test is sometimes referred to as a contingency analysis (Bajpai, 2011)

The hypothesis testing procedure for the Chi-Square test will be as follows:

1. **Set the Null hypothesis**

   That is the two or more variables are independent of each other

2. **Determine the appropriate test statistics**

3. **Set the level of significance.**

   Generally, it is the 0.05 significance level. The Excel software is by default set on this.

In Excel, the chi-square value will be significant if the resulted p-value output using the function **'chisq.test'** comes out to below 0.05.

4. **Set the decision rule**

   If the chi-squared calculated value is greater than the critical value from the table. Reject the null hypothesis.

5. **Collect the sample data**

6. **Analyze the data**

7. **Accepting or rejecting the Null hypothesis and Interpreting its meaning for the business world.**

Calculating the Chi-Square Test

Develop the contingency table with variables (f_0-observed frequencies) arranged in rows and columns, e.g. as shown in the table below, one variable in a row and another in a column such that a matrix is formed.

Example:

Calculate row and column total.

Age\Brand	Brand 1	Brand 2	Brand 3	Row Total
Age group 1	10	15	15	40
Age group 2	20	20	10	50
Age group 3	30	25	25	80
Column Total	60	60	50	180 (Make sure your row and column total should be same)

*Example to make a contingency table

Calculate expected frequencies (fe) for each variable.

fe $(1,1)$ = RT*CT/N

Here fe $(1,1)$ = Expected frequency for variable at $(1,1)$ location, RT= Row Total, CT=Column total and N is total number of samples.

100 A Concise Handbook of Business Research

Calculate the degree of freedom which is (Number of Rows -1)* (Number of Columns -1)

Draw a table of observed frequencies, expected frequencies, and observed expected frequencies 'χ^2'.

chi-square value is shown as

'χ^2' = $(f_o - f_e)^2/f_e$

If the value of chi-square calculated is significant at the set confidence interval that is, it is above the table value of chi-square test the null hypothesis is rejected. Else we say that we fail to reject the null hypothesis if the chi-square value is less than the table value of the chi-square test.

Q1. A company wants to check whether the use of its soap brand consumption is dependent on gender (among males and females) or not. For this, the company collected 100 samples to measure it. The frequency table is shown below. Use a Chi-square test to reach the desired result.

Soap	Male	Female	Row Total
S1	10	20	30
S2	10	5	15
S3	20	5	25
S4	10	20	30
Column Total	50	50	100

We set the null hypothesis that the consumption of the soaps brand is independent of gender. Here we put our significance level to 0.05. and set criteria that if the calculated value of chi-square comes significant i.e. if the p-value output comes using 'chisq.test' function comes less than 0.05 than the null hypothesis will be rejected.

Calculating the Chi-Square test manually.

First, we need to calculate the expected frequencies (table 4.7).

Table 4.7: Calculating Expected Frequencies in Chi-Square Test

Expected frequencies		
Soap	Male	Female
S1	15	15
S2	7.5	7.5
S3	12.5	12.5
S4	15	15

For S1 the value of male comes out to be 50*30/100=15. For S2 the value of male comes out to be 50*15/100=7.5.... and similarly, calculate the expected frequencies using the method given above.

Calculate the degree of freedom which is (Number of Rows -1)* (Number of Columns -1)

$= (4 - 1)* (2 - 1)$

$=3*1$

$=3$ is the degree of freedom

Now develop the table having Observed frequencies (f_0), Expected frequencies (f_e), $(f_0 - f_e)$, $(f_0 - f_e)^2$, $(f_0 - f_e)^2/f_e$.

Table 4.8: Calculating Chi Square Value Manually

Observed frequencies (f_0)	Expected frequencies (f_e)	$f_e - f_0$	$(f_e - f_0)^2$	$(f_e - f_0)^2/f_e$
10	15	−5	25	1.667
10	7.5	2.5	6.25	0.833
20	12.5	7.5	56.25	4.500
10	15	−5	25	1.667
20	15	5	25	1.667
5	7.5	−2.5	6.25	0.833
5	12.5	−7.5	56.25	4.500
20	15	5	25	1.667
Sum (Chi-Square cal.)				17.333

102 A Concise Handbook of Business Research

At a 95% confidence level with 03 degrees of freedom, the critical value of χ2 calculated is 17.33 which is more than χ2 table value of 7.8417 χ2 (See the table in appendices). *Hence, we reject the null hypothesis,* i.e. there is enough evidence to indicate that the consumption of soaps is affected by gender.

Chi-Square Test Using Excel

Performing chi-square test in excel requires the use of the function '*CHISQ.TEST ()*'.

First, write the observed and expected frequencies in two columns in the excel sheet. Then on the topmost pane go to 'formulas', then to 'more function', then select '*CHISQ.TEST*'. Select the actual range (observed values range) and the expected range. When you select and hit enter the value comes out is a p-value. *If it is less than 0.05 then you can reject your null hypothesis.*

Here in our case the output of 'chisq.test= 0.015369' which is below the 0.05 significance level set. Hence, we reject the null hypothesis and reach the conclusion that soap brands preference is dependent on gender.

Calculating the Chi-Square Test in R

Let us reconfigure the data set we used above for excel. Here due to limited space, it is in five columns, but in the excel sheet make it only in two columns, the Soap type, and the Gender.

Soap Type	Gender	Soap Type	Gender	Soap Type	Gender	Soap Type	Gender	Soap Type	Gender
S1	Male	S3	Male	S4	Male	S1	Female	S4	Female
S1	Male	S3	Male	S4	Male	S1	Female	S4	Female
S1	Male	S3	Male	S4	Male	S1	Female	S4	Female
S1	Male	S3	Male	S4	Male	S1	Female	S4	Female
S1	Male	S3	Male	S4	Male	S1	Female	S4	Female
S1	Male	S3	Male	S4	Male	S1	Female	S4	Female
S1	Male	S3	Male	S4	Male	S1	Female	S4	Female
S1	Male	S3	Male	S4	Male	S1	Female	S4	Female
S1	Male	S3	Male	S4	Male	S1	Female	S4	Female
S1	Male	S3	Male	S4	Male	S1	Female	S4	Female

Contd...

Data and Method of Analysis 103

Soap Type	Gender	Soap Type	Gender	Soap Type	Gender	Soap Type	Gender	Soap Type	Gender
S2	Male	S3	Male	S1	Female	S4	Female	S3	Female
S2	Male	S3	Male	S1	Female	S4	Female	S3	Female
S2	Male	S3	Male	S1	Female	S4	Female	S3	Female
S2	Male	S3	Male	S1	Female	S4	Female	S3	Female
S2	Male	S3	Male	S1	Female	S4	Female	S3	Female
S2	Male	S3	Male	S1	Female	S4	Female	S2	Female
S2	Male	S3	Male	S1	Female	S4	Female	S2	Female
S2	Male	S3	Male	S1	Female	S4	Female	S2	Female
S2	Male	S3	Male	S1	Female	S4	Female	S2	Female
S2	Male	S3	Male	S1	Female	S4	Female	S2	Female

This is the list of 100 samples collected to measure whether there is an association between gender and soap type. Whether the consumption of soaps is affected by gender. Make sure there are only two variables.

Use the following commands to produce Chi-Square test output in R.

Output of R

```
> AA<-read.csv("dep.chi.csv")
> str(AA)
'data.frame':100 obs. of 2 variables:
$ Soap  : Factor w/ 4 levels "S1", "S2", "S3",..: 1 1 1 1 1 1 1 1 1 1 ...
$ Gender: Factor w/ 2 levels "Female", "Male": 2 2 2 2 2 2 2 2 2 2 ...
> table(AA$Soap, AA$Gender)
Female Male
S1    20   10
S2     5   10
S3     5   20
S4    20   10
> table.chi<-table(AA$Soap, AA$Gender)
> chisq.test(table.chi)
Pearson's Chi-squared test
data:  table.chi
X-squared = 17.333, df = 3, p-value = 0.0006035
```

104 A Concise Handbook of Business Research

Here we have performed some new operations for you. So that your learning can be improved by using R.

Firstly, you might be seeing this command "AA<-read.csv("dep.chi. csv")". This command means that a file in *'.csv'* format is created, a format well suited for 'R' to work on. You could have directly loaded excel file where you have feed your data on this question. But we saw that in excel format we had to change few variables from character to factors to make some operations successful. Whereas in R it automatically reads the type of variable used (in most cases). Then after reading the file, we saved it to variable AA for further use. To convert an excel file to .csv file just save the excel file in '.csv' format, known as comma separated file. *"Consult your class teacher if you are not able to do so".*

Using 'str(AA)' command we got clear what type of variables we are having. For the chi-square test, we need both variables as factors. Seeing in the above table both the variables are factors.

Then we used 'table (AA$Soap, AA$Gender) command to get their frequencies. We can see clearly that in term of soap consumption how it is distributed between males and females.

After this, we used 'table.chi<-table(AA$Soap, AA$Gender)' to save the output of table function in the variable 'table.chi'. it makes our work bit easier to work with small name structure.

And lastly, we used the function 'chisq.test(table.chi)' to get the chi-square test. The output shows that chi-square value is = 17.333, with the degree of freedom = 3, and p-value = 0.0006035. Since our P-value is significant and is below 0.05 (a default significance level) we reach to a conclusion that the chi-square statistics is significant, and there is a significant difference between male and female consumption of these four types of soaps category.

Correlation and Regression Analysis

Correlation and regression are important tools in research for studying relationships between variables, and for building statistical models.

Correlation

Correlation in statistics is a measure of how close two variables are to have a linear relationship (change in the value of one variable produces change in the value of another variable) with each other. An important assumption of correlation analysis is that the variables must have a linear relationship with one another.

In common usage, Pearson's Correlations Coefficient is used as a measure of correlation between two variables. There are other less commonly used correlation measures such as Spearman's Rank Order Correlation Coefficient, and Kendall's Rank Order Coefficient, which we will touch upon in brief in this chapter.

Pearson's Correlation Coefficient

Pearson's Correlation Coefficient (denoted 'r') indicates the degree of linear association between two continuous variables. The value of Pearson's Correlation Coefficient ranges from -1 to +1, a positive value of Pearson's Correlation Coefficient indicates a positive association between two variables, while a negative value of 'r' indicates a negative association. When 'r' is positive it means, as the value of one variable increases the value on the other variable also increases. The reserve is the case when 'r' is negative. Values of 'r' close to 0, indicate no correlation.

Assumptions to Check for Pearson's Correlation

- Variables should be measured on an interval or ratio scale (continuous variable)
- There should be a linear relationship between the variables.
- Data should not contain outliers.
- Data should be normally distributed.

Q: Estimate Pearson's Correlation for the two variables (X and Y) using Excel and R.

X	Y
23	18
21	20

X	Y
23	22
28	27
22	21
30	29
29	27
33	29
24	22
26	21

Estimating Pearson's Correlation Coefficient in Excel

The process for estimating Pearson's correlation in Excel is very simple. After entering the data in excel, go to the data tab and click on the data analysis button at the end of the ribbon. A dialog box will appear, select "correlation" in that and click "ok" (Fig 4.30).

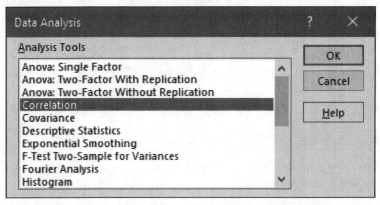

Fig. 4.30: Data Analysis Dialogue Box for Correlation

Next, we need to select the columns that have the data for the variables for which the correlation needs to be calculated, the columns are selected by highlighting them. When we click on the "input range" box in the correlation window, it will automatically switch to the worksheet view. The correlation dialog box prompts the user to select these columns (Fig. 4.31). Make sure to select the "labels in the first row" checkbox. After this just click "ok". A new worksheet will open and show the output (Table 1). From Table 1 we can see that the estimated correlation coefficient is 0.9085586, this indicates that X and Y have a high degree of positive correlation between them.

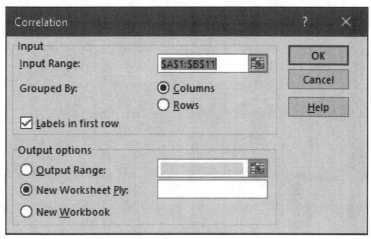

Fig. 4.31 Correlation Dialog Box

Table 4.9: Correlation Analysis Output in Excel

	X	Y
X	1	
Y	0.908586	1

Estimating Pearson's Correlation Coefficient in R

For estimating "r", the cor () function is used. The general syntax is as follows:

cor (variable1, variable2, method = "pearson")

In conjunction with the cor () function, the cor.test () function is also used. The cor.test () function outputs the significance (p-value) of the correlation coefficient as well confidence level estimates. The general syntax for cor.test () is:

cor.test (variable1, variable2)

The cor () function is quite self-explanatory. The first two arguments are basically the names of the variables for which a correlation coefficient

108 A Concise Handbook of Business Research

is desired. Lastly, the "method" argument basically tells the function which method of calculating correlation should be used. For the majority of the cases, this argument is set to "pearson". The cor.test () function is also quite simple to use, we just mention the name of the variable for which the correlation significance is desired. However, one does not necessarily need to calculate the significance (p-value) associated with correlation coefficients as the correlation coefficient is just an "effect size". The following R script can be used for this task:

#vectors for storing data

x<-c(23,21,23,28,22,30,29,33,24,26)

we are creating a list of numbers and then saving it in a variable.

y<-c(18,20,22,27,21,29,27,29,22,21)

shapiro.test(x)# for testing for normality

shapiro.test(y)

cor(x, y, method = "pearson")

Output of R

shapiro.test(x)# for testing for normality

Shapiro-Wilk normality test

data: x

W = 0.93805, p-value = 0.5315

> shapiro.test(y)

Shapiro-Wilk normality test

data: y

W = 0.88341, p-value = 0.1428

> cor(x, y, method = "pearson")

[1] 0.9085857

Let us now interpret the R output.

The first part of the output prints out the results of the *Shapiro-Wilk test for normality*. The p-values of the Shapiro-Wilk test for both the variables are greater than 0.05 (0.53, 0.14), which indicates that the data is normally distributed. Thus, the assumption of normality for Pearson's correlation coefficient is not violated. The next part of the output prints out the correlation coefficient, which comes out to be 0.9085.

For a more detailed discussion on correlation analysis and other correlation estimation methods such as Spearman's and Kendall's coefficient refer to Nath (2018).

Linear Regression Analysis (OLS Regression)

In the field of statistics, regression analysis is a set of statistical procedures for estimating relationships among variables. To simply put, regression analysis helps in understanding how the value of a dependent variable (or 'criterion variable') changes when one or more of the independent variables is varied. The term regression analysis is mostly used for referring to the "ordinary least square" (OLS) method of doing regression analysis. There are other methods of doing regression analysis, such as logistics, polynomial, lasso and ridge regression. Nevertheless, the current text-only focuses on regression analysis using the OLS approach. Regression analysis is a very powerful tool in statistics that can do many tasks such as, hypothesis testing, inferring causality and for making predictions.

Important Terms Associated with Regression Analysis

Before proceeding further with conducting a regression analysis, it is imperative to understand certain terms, which will come repeatedly in the course of using regression analysis.

- Regression Model: The basic linear regression model is represented through an equation of a straight line:

  $Y = mX + c + e$

  Where Y is the dependent variable

X is the independent variable

m is the coefficient of the independent variable (also known as regression coefficient or beta coefficient)

c is the intercept (also known as the regression constant). This is the point where the regression line/plane cuts the y-axis.

e is the error term.

- Dependent and Independent Variables: To simply put, a dependent variable is the one, whose value depends on other variables. It is the variable, which is getting affected by some other variables. In the above regression equation, Y is the dependent variable.

  An independent variable as its name suggests is some variable whose value is not dependent on any other variables in the regression model. The variable affects the value of the dependent variable. In the above regression equation, X is the independent variable. A Dependent variable is also known by other names such as output variable, criterion variable, outcome variable. An independent variable is also known by various names such as predictor variable, explanatory variable.

- The lower-case letter "m" in the above regression equation is the regression coefficient of the independent variable "x". The regression coefficient represents the rate of change in Y i.e. the dependent variable as the value of X i.e. the independent variable changes. That is to say, "m" is the slope of the regression line.

  Readers who are interested in reading in depth about regression analysis can refer to Nath (2018).

The assumption of Linear Regression Analysis

- A Linear Relationship Between The Dependent and The Independent Variable(s).
- The Assumption of Normality.
- Data Should Not Contain Any Outliers.
- Data Should be Measured on an Interval or Ratio Scale.

Regression Analysis using Excel

For understanding regression analysis we need a dataset. For this we have used a dataset 'LungCapData.xls' downloaded from the website, https://sites.google.com/site/rusersguide/.The data set contains 725 observations and is about lung capacity of a person based on different factors.

The process for estimating Pearson's correlation in Excel is very simple. After entering the data go to the data tab and click on the data analysis button at the end of the ribbon. A dialog box will appear, select "correlation" in that and click "ok" (Fig 4.32).

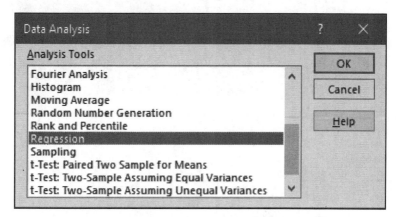

Fig. 4.32 Regression in Data Analysis Dialog Box

Next, we need to select the columns that have the data for the variables for which the correlation needs to be calculated, the columns are selected by highlighting them (Fig. 4.33).

When we click on the "input range Y" box in the regression window, it will automatically switch to the worksheet view. The "input range Y" box, asks for the column where the data for the dependent variable is placed. And "input range X" box asks for the columns where the data for the independent variables is placed. Make sure to select the "labels in the first row" checkbox and then select the appropriate confidence level. After this click "ok". Hitting ok will produce a table 4.10.

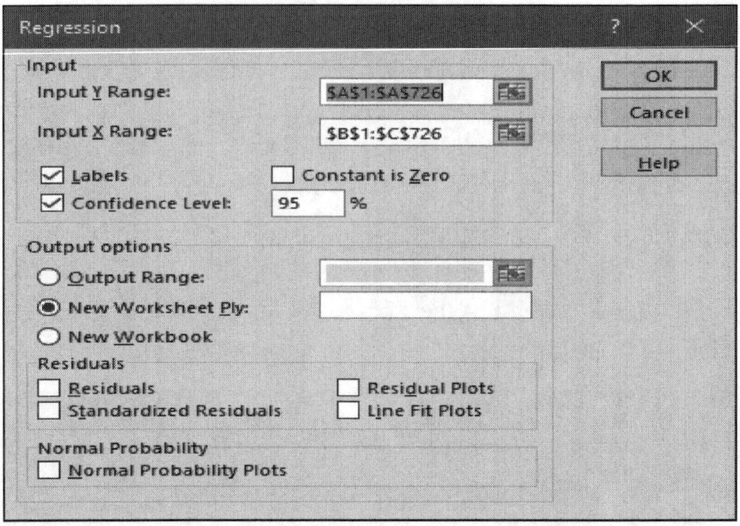

112 A Concise Handbook of Business Research

Fig. 4.33 Regression Analysis Dialog Box

Table 4.10: Regression Analysis Output from Excel

SUMMARY OUTPUT									
Regression Statistics									
Multiple R	0.918142								
R Square	0.842984								
Adjusted R Square	0.842549								
Standard Error	1.056287								
Observations	725								
ANOVA	df	SS	MS	F	Signifi-cance F				
Regression	2	4324.906	2162.453	1938.129	5.4E-291				
Residual	722	805.5663	1.115743						
Total	724	5130.472							
	Coeffi-cients	Standard Error	t Stat	P-value	Lower 95%	Upper 95%	Lower 95.0%	Upper 95.0%	
Intercept	-11.7471	0.476899	-24.6322	1.03E-97	-12.6833	-10.8108	-12.6833	-10.8108	
age	0.126368	0.017851	7.07906	3.45E-12	0.091322	0.161414	0.091322	0.161414	
height	0.278432	0.009926	28.05067	1.1E-117	0.258945	0.297919	0.258945	0.297919	

The interpretation is discussed along with output produced by R.

Calculating Regression Analysis Using R

Using the data file (lungcap.csv), taking age and height as an independent variable and lung capacity as a dependent variable to conduct a regression analysis and test the hypotheses that age and height have no significant effect on lung capacity.

The following R script can be used for this task:

```
mydata<-read.csv(file.choose(), header = T)
library(QuantPsyc)
mymodel<-lm (lungCap~age+height, data=mydata)
summary (mymodel)
modelbeta<-lm.beta (mymodel)
print (modelbeta)
```

Output of R

Call the function:

lm (formula = lungCap ~ age + height, data = mydata)

Residuals:

Min	1Q	Median	3Q	Max
−3.4080	−0.7097	−0.0078	0.7167	3.1679

Coefficients:

	Estimate	Std. Error	t value	Pr(>|t|)	
(Intercept)	−11.747065	0.476899	−24.632	< 2e-16	***
age	0.126368	0.017851	7.079	3.45e-12	***
height	0.278432	0.009926	28.051	< 2e-16	***

Signif. codes: 0 '***' 0.001 '**' 0.01 '*' 0.05 '.' 0.1 ' ' 1

Residual standard error: 1.056 on 722 degrees of freedom

Multiple R-squared: 0.843,

Adjusted R-squared: 0.8425

114   A Concise Handbook of Business Research

F-statistic: 1938 on 2 and 722 DF, p-value: < 2.2e-16

> modelbeta <-lm.beta (mymodel)

> print (modelbeta)

age   height

0.1901094   0.7533059

The output of the regression analysis first shows the residuals (min: –3.4, median –0.007, max: 3.16). From the output, it is evident that the residuals are quite symmetrical.

Secondly, the coefficients of the independent variables are shown. Age has a coefficient of 0.126368 (t = 7.079, p = 0.000) and height has a coefficient of 0.278432 (t = 28.051, p = 0.000), their respective standardized coefficients are 0.1901094 and 0.7533059. Since coefficients of both age and height are statistically significant ($p < 0.05$), we will have to look at their magnitude. The standardized coefficient for height (0.7533059) is greater than that of age (0.1901094). Thus, height has a more significant positive (as coefficients are positive) effect on lung capacity as compared to age.

Lastly, the model R^2 is mentioned along with the adjusted R^2, which are 0.843 and 0.8425 respectively. Since, both the predictors are significant. Therefore, there is not much difference between the values of R^2 and adjusted R^2, as adjusted R^2 gets reduced in comparison to R^2, due to the presence of independent variables which have an insignificant coefficient.

To conclude, the overall model fit is reported with F = 1930 at df: 2 and 722 with p=.000, which indicates, that regression model fits the data quite well, and thus, on a whole age and height effect lung capacity.

Notice that in comparison to example 5.3, the R^2 value of this model has increased from 0.6719 to 0.843, which means that age along with height can account for 84.3% variation in lung capacity. So, in this case, adding one more independent variable has improved the model.

Thus, age and height significantly affect lung capacity.

For a more detailed discussion on regression analysis and refer to Nath (2018).

4.3.3 Multivariate Analysis

Factor Analysis

While conducting research on a particular topic you may deal with multiple variables. One of the most important insights in dealing with multiple variables is the relationship between variables which gets more complicated as the number of variables in the study increases (Example if in a movie there is one hero, one heroine and one villain it is quite simple to predict what will happen. However, if the same movie had more closely related characters, the picture had become more complicated.

To understand the relationship among variables in this complex structure of multiple variables statisticians has developed two core techniques for grouping of variables.

Principal Component Analysis (PCA): Which deals with reducing the number of variables from many to few. It is based on the concept that if the variables are closely related and show a good correlation, they can be combined and reduced to a few variables. In the production subject, we have a saying that simple designs with few components are easy to work on than complicated design with many components.

Exploratory Factor Analysis (EFA): When grouping variables on the basis of close association among them (based on correlation matrix) we may come up with few variables which are grouped together such that they together make a sense of a latent variable or a factor. This latent variable is a hidden variable which comes into picture when we see two or more variables relating such that they together make a sense and can be presented by a new name.

Example of PCA and EFA

Let us just assume an example to make the concept of PCA and EFA clear. Suppose you are studying about leadership behavior of production supervisor based on past studies. You took 20 traits shown by leaders and collected the data on it by 1000 supervisors.

First, you run EFA and see how the 20 variables are group together. This is achieved by seeing the degree of correlation or association among variables. However, in doing so if you find that out of 20 variables there are 08 variables group together on one side and 08 variables grouped together one another side. You can sense that broadly there might be two variables, let us say, employee-oriented supervisors and production-oriented supervisors. But there are still 04 variables which are out from the first group as well as a second group and are showing association. And if you combine them together, they make sense. You may name this third grouping as a third leadership behavior that is "In the middle of the road". Here we got three latent variables now: Employee oriented, production oriented and middle of the road.

However, at times you might just be interested in reducing the number of variables because they are too much and are closely relate,d you may use PCA because the objective is not to find a latent variable but to reduce the variables to few. Example student's performance can be evaluated on many parameters say we take 05 factors initially: Class Attendance, Internal, Marks, External Marks, Class Participation, Assignments, Projects. If we run PCA and find internal and external marks closely associated we make combine them together and reduce two into a single factor called as 'Marks' and reducing the data set to 04 variables.

The technique of factor analysis has three main uses (field, A., 2012):

- To understand the set of variables (A latent variable)
- In the construction of a questionnaire by understanding the set of variables.

- In reducing the complexity of the model by simplifying the design i.e. reducing the variables such that the information of the overall structure is still retained.

However as said by Field (2012), the basic use of factor analysis is purely exploratory which is about understanding the structure of data i.e. how the variables are clustered together.

The common steps to perform PCA or EFA as mentioned by Kabacoff (2011) are mentioned below:

Step1: Produce a correlation matrix on your variables.

Step 2: Select whether you want to reduce variables or to explore factors. If you want to reduce variable use PCA and if you want to explore factors or you think some new factors can be explored run EFA.

Step 3: Decide how many factors to be extracted.

Step4: Extract the factors.

Step 5: Rotating (grouping) the factors so that they can be classified into two or three or more factors as decided into step2.

Step 6: Interpret the results

Step 7: Compute the score of the factors.

Researchers use these steps most often to validate their questionnaire i.e. it should measure what it is made up for. We call it "factor analysis to validate your questionnaire".

Researchers after validity, check the reliability of the questionnaire. Reliability reflects that the questionnaire is measuring the same thing every time it is used.

Discriminant Analysis

Discriminant Analysis is a technique used by researchers when the dependent variable is in categorical form and not in interval or ratio scale (Bajpai, 2011). Normally to check dependence of one variable over another we use regression analysis. When the number of variables

118 A Concise Handbook of Business Research

independent side increases, we call it a multiple regression analysis. But in regression analysis, we have both the sides of equation (independent and dependent variables) on interval or ratio scale. However, when the dependent variable is of a categorical nature, we cannot use the simple regression analysis. For this, we use the Discriminant Analysis.

Let me give you a hi-fi definition by (Hoare, 2017) which is useful when you talk in terms of data analytics

"Linear Discriminant Analysis (LDA) is a well-established machine learning technique for predicting categories."

He says that the LDA algorithm (or the set of steps) uses the data to divide the space of predictor variables (independent variables) into regions or categories (dependent variable). The model predicts the category of a new unseen case according to which region it lies in. The model predicts that all cases within a region belong to the same category.

Performing Discriminant Analysis or Linear Discriminant Analysis using R

Here are the steps are taken from (www.statmethods.net, n.d.):

Step 1: Install the package "MASS"

Step 2: Load the package "MASS"

Step 3: lda(dependent variable ~ Independent variable 1+ Independent variable 2+....., data = data.frame, na.action = "na.omit", CV=TRUE) **step 4:** performs the actual linear discriminant analysis. Here the dependent variable is a factor variable and independent variables are on interval or ratio scale.

Tentative Exam Questions

1. What is software R? How it is beneficial for research students.
2. Explain the procedure for working on an excel file in R.
3. Explain the procedure for installing the data analysis pack in Excel.

Data and Method of Analysis 119

4. What is ANOVA? Differentiate between One-way and Two-way ANOVA.

5. What is Chi-Square Test? For what purpose it is used.

6. Define correlation and regression analysis.

7. Define factor analysis.

8. Define Discriminant analysis.

❑❑❑

5

Improving Academic Writing

> **Syllabus Unit 5:** *Improving your academic writing; Referencing and citation in MS word., Plagiarism, its Detection, and Removal. Introduction to Grammarly. Tentative Exam questions.*

5.1 Referencing and In-text Citation

Citation and referencing in research writing (or academic writing) is about giving credit to the person whose material we have used or are using for our research work. Throughout the journey of this book, you might have seen that wherever we have used other's work we have mentioned the source of it. This is called as citation. This citation needs to be documented comprehensively in detail, which comes under the 'Bibliography/References or Work Cited' section. The complete details of the work to be cited include the name of the author, year of publication, the title of the research work cited, journal/book name, issue, volume, from where is it published, online link and other important details. This section is generally at the end pages of your research work (before the appendices section, depending on the style your supervisor or your university is preferring).

(121)

122 A Concise Handbook of Business Research

5.1.1 Adding In-text Citation and References in MS-Word 2016

For writing this book we have used MS word 2016. MS-word contains citation and referencing option. So, let us start the process.

Open your research work file which is in MS-Word format. See the top ribbon of it. Next to 'Home', 'Insert', 'Design', 'Layout' icons, you may find **'References'**. Click on it.

Now the ribbon shows broad icons as 'Table of contents', 'Footnotes', **'Citation and Bibliography'**, 'Captions', 'Index' and 'Table of Authorities'.

Now see the **Citation and Bibliography** section in detail. It contains four sections in it: **Insert Citation, Manage Sources, Style and Bibliography.**

The first thing you need to look here is **'Style'. Here you got many different styles of writing citation and references.** Two of the styles most prevalent among Indian Universities and other International universities are **'APA'** which is a style by the American Psychological Association and the second is Harvard -Anglia by Harvard. APA sixth style has been used for this book. Now start by first setting style recommended by your university.

Now click on **'Insert Citation'**. Here you may see two options **'Add new source' and 'Add new placeholder'**. Click on **'Add new source'** and start with your first citation journey. Click on this and it will open up a new window **'Create Source', visible on the top left of the black ribbon strip.** Let me explain the process and key terms further using a citation example (Creswell, 2017) which we used in the first chapter.

Now moving further, you may find first option **'Type of Source'.** Now the work which you may be citing may be a **Book, Book section, Journal article, Article in a periodical, Conference proceeding, Report, Website, Document from the website, Electronic source, Art, Sound recording, Performance, Film, Interview, Patent, Case or Miscellaneous.** Click on that option which fits best for your citing work. In my case, it is a book.

'Then add author name. Here in 'Author' section, an icon is of 'edit', click on it. A new window will pop up. Add the last name, middle name and first name of the author, for example for John Creswell, the last name will be Creswell, middle name will be W. and the first name John.

Improving Academic Writing 123

Add more details by clicking on the icon 'Show all Bibliography Fields'. When you are done with this, click ok and your citation will appear like (Creswell, 2017). Like this add citation wherever you require to support your work or wherever you are using someone else published work. Talk to your subject teacher on this further.

After adding all citations to your work go to the main 'Citation and bibliography' section (which if you have not forgotten is on the top of word page under references section on the top ribbon of MS word page.) Now click on its another section, '**Bibliography**'. This section is about adding '**References**' which comes at the end of the book or the chapter. When you click on the Bibliography section different options pop up like **Bibliography, References and Work Cited**. The bibliography is about citing all secondary resources you consult for your research work, even if you did not cite that work. Whereas References and Work Cited are related to citing of only those secondary sources in your work which you have used as In-text citation. For managing your citation and references use the section '**Manage Sources**'.

Now Let me show you the process of citation and references with images: First image is about opening insert citation, then adding citation content, authors details, then clicking the bibliography section to get the references list (see fig. 5.1, 5.2, 5.3,5.4).

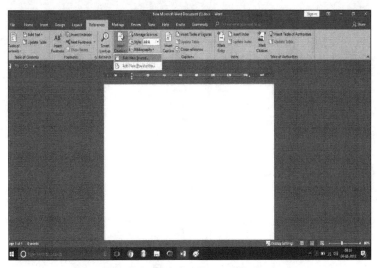

Fig. 5.1: Opening 'Insert Citation'

124 A Concise Handbook of Business Research

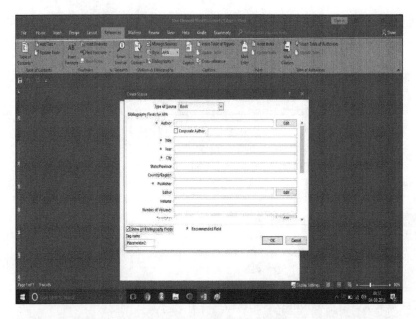

Fig. 5.2: Adding Citation Content in MS-Word

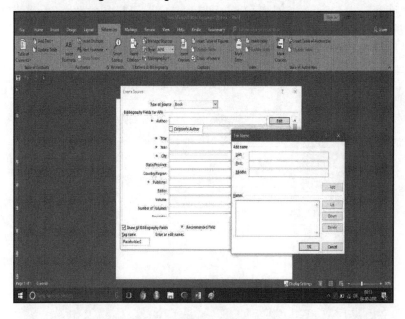

Fig. 5.3: Adding Author Details

Improving Academic Writing 125

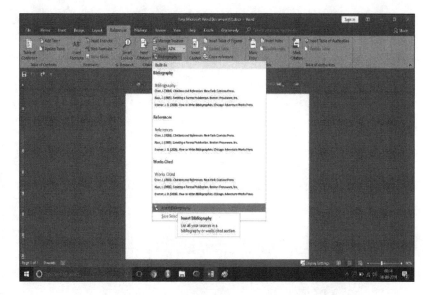

Fig. 5.4: Generating Bibliography Section

In summary, to work on your citation and references section, you need to first add in-text citation wherever you use any secondary source. Make sure you are clear with the style to use like that of APA or Harvard, MLA etc. When you have completed all in-text citation in your work then click on bibliography section, and your references list will be generated which will appear at the end pages of your research work, like that of this book in the references section.

5.2 Plagiarism, What it is? How to Detect? and How-to Remove?

As defined in the notification by University Grants Commission (Promotion of Academic Integrity and Prevention of Plagiarism in Higher Educational Institutions) Regulations, 2018, '**Plagiarism**' is defined as "The practice of taking someone else work or idea and passing them as your own.". This practice of coping should be strictly avoided in any research work, whether it a BBA project work, MBA Dissertation work or Ph.D. thesis work.

126 A Concise Handbook of Business Research

UGC has issued guidelines for this especially for students doing their Dissertations and Thesis. The summary of the acceptable level of plagiarism and related penalties mentioned by UGC are given below (UGC, 2018):

I. **Level Zero: Similarities of work up to 10%** - Here similarity means your work which is similar to already published work. Under 10% plagiarism will be considered under minor similarity and there will be no penalty on it.

II. **Level One: Similarities of work above 10% to 40%** - In this case students need to revise and resubmit their work within a given time frame not exceeding 06 months.

III. **Level Two: Similarities of work above 40% to 60%** - In this case, the penalty is much severe and may lead to debarring of the student for one year.

IV. **Level Three: Similarities of work above 60%** -In this case where the plagiarism level is so high the candidate registration may be cancelled.

For more details read the complete document https://www.ugc.ac.in/pdfnews/7771545_academic-integrity-Regulation2018.pdf

5.2.1 Plagiarism Detection and Removal

To detect the plagiarism in your work you need a good plagiarism detection software.

The most trustworthy and used internationally is **Turnitin** (go to https://guides.turnitin.com/01_Manuals_and_Guides/Instructor_Guides/Turnitin_Classic_(Deprecated)/21_The_Similarity_Report/Viewing_the_Similarity_Report) to understand how Turnitin works on your assignments.

Other than Turnitin there are few software more like **URKUND** and **no.plagiate.de**. The last one is free but the quality produced by Turnitin is of the highest order.

Once the plagiarism is detected by the software, a report is generated by it clearly describing which lines in your research work looks very similar to other's work. Two things you can do to remove similarities found:

Delete that work which is very similar or Improve your work by rewriting the lines or paragraph which is similar to others work.

5.3 Improve Your Academic Writing Using Free Software Grammarly

Grammarly is an artificial intelligence-based software used by millions of users worldwide to improve their writing. It works by detecting the writing errors like contextual spelling, grammar, sentence structure, style, punctuation, vocabulary, in your word file. It is available in both a free and paid version. The free version covers basic spelling, grammar, punctuation, sentence structure, and style correction. Whereas the premium or the paid version covers the advance issues, genre, vocabulary enhancement, and plagiarism check. Go to the website **www.grammarly.com** and install it. You need to first log in and then the different download options start. We have installed its two options out of three depending on our needs: google chrome and MS-Office. For word document, when you are done with installation its icon will appear on the word document page. Click on that '**Grammarly**' icon, then click the '**Open Grammarly**' icon to work with it.

While processing it, a Grammarly window appears on the right-hand side. Scroll your document down or scroll down the Grammarly window to see the writing part which requires correction. The words or sentences which require corrections start appearing in red and green. Click on the items on the right-hand side window and improve your writing. To under its function see the snapshots below.

128 A Concise Handbook of Business Research

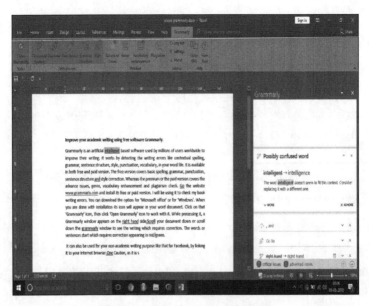

Fig. 5.5: Grammarly for Windows

Just one caution, as it is still a computer so it needs your judgment too. Check each and every word which it marks in your writing.

You can also take advantage of its some additional features like plagiarism detection (which is again a very good asset of Grammarly), vocabulary, and other advance writing issues, but for that you have to convert that into the payed version. Quillbot is another software used for improved academic writing. Do visit the website of the software.

Tentative Exam Questions

1. What is the role of citation in academic writing?
2. Explain the procedure for citing work in the text in the MS-Word file.
3. What is plagiarism? What is the minimum acceptable level as per UGC guidelines? How to remove it.
4. What is Grammarly? How it is useful in academic writing.

❑❑❑

References

1. Advisors, R. (2018). *Sample size.* Retrieved from www.research-advisors.com: https://www.research-advisors.com/tools/SampleSize.htm

2. Anand, P. (2016, March). *Impact and Implications of workplace loneliness: A two sample mixed method study.* Retrieved from www.shodhganga.inflibnet.ac.in/.

3. Bajpai, N. (2011). *Business Research methods.* New Delhi: Pearson Education.

4. Blumberg, B., Cooper, D. R., & Schindler, P. S. (2005). *Business Research Methods.* New Delhi: Mc-GrawHill.

5. Creswell, J. W. (2014). *Research Design:4th ed.* CA: Sage.

6. Creswell, J. W. (2017). *Education Research: Planning, Conducting, and Evaluating Quantitative and Qualitative Research.* Noida: Pearson India.

7. Crotty, M. (1998). *The foundation of social research: Meaning and perspective in the research process.* Thousand Oaks, CA: Sage.

8. Crotty, M. (1998). *The foundation of social research: Meaning and perspective in the research process.* London: Sage.

9. Dangi, H. K. (2012, April). performance Management of Distribution Management After Natural Disaster. *Ph.D. Thesis.* Shodhganga. Retrieved from http://shodhganga.inflibnet.ac.in/handle/10603/28369

10. *Data Analysis Using R.* (2019). Retrieved from https://in.udacity.com: https://in.udacity.com/course/data-analysis-with-r-ud651

11. Denzin, N. K. (2011). *The SAGE Handbook of qualitative research.* CA`: Sage.

(129)

12. Goforth, C. (2015, November 16). *Research Data Services*. Retrieved from http://data.library.virginia.edu/: http://data.library.virginia.edu/using-and-interpreting-cronbachs-alpha/

13. Guda Vasudeva, R. (2016). A frame work for performance measurement of Indian Small and Medium Size enterprises SMES an operations view. Indore, MP, India. Retrieved from http://shodhganga.inflibnet.ac.in: http://shodhganga.inflibnet.ac.in/handle/10603/88960

14. Hamming, R. (2016, March 07). *You and Your Research'*. Retrieved from www.me.iitb.ac.in: www.me.iitb.ac.in/~dmarla/Richard_Hamming.pdf

15. Hinkin, T. R. (1995). A review of scale development practices in the study of organizations. *Journal of Management, 21*(5), 967-988.

16. Hinkin, T. R. (2005). Scale development principles and practices. *Research in organizations:Foundations & methods of inquiry*, 161-179.

17. Hoare, J. (2017, 10 11). *linear-discriminant-analysis-in-r-an-introduction*. Retrieved from https://www.r-bloggers.com/: https://www.r-bloggers.com/linear-discriminant-analysis-in-r-an-introduction/

18 *http://global.shopnielsen.com/reports/region-india*. (2018). Retrieved from http://www.nielsen.com: http://global.shopnielsen.com/reports/region-india

19. Jitarani, U. (2013). Development of a framework for International Marketing Strategy a study of Indian Shrimps Prawns. *PhD Thesis*. Retrieved from http://shodhganga.inflibnet.ac.in: http://hdl.handle.net/10603/6695.

20. Kabacoff, R. I. (2011). *R in Action:Data analysis and graphics with R*. NY: Manning Publications.

21. KhanAcademy. (n.d.). *analysis-of-variance-anova-library*. Retrieved from https://www.khanacademy.org/: https://www.khanacademy.org/math/statistics-probability/analysis-of-variance-anova-library.

22. Kothari, C. R. (2004). *Research Methodology*. New Delhi: New Age.

References   131

23. Machi, L. A., & McEvoy, B. T. (2016). *The Literature Review:Six steps to success.* (3rd. ed.). California: Corwin.

24. Osgood, C. (1964). Semantic Differential Technique in the Comparative Study of Cultures. *American Anthropologist, 66*(3), 171-200. doi:http://www.jstor.org/stable/669329.

25. Panneerselvam, R. (2012). *Research Methodology.* New Delhi: PHI.

26. Patton, M. Q. (2015, Jan. 23). Literature Reviews: Common Errors Made When Conducting a Literature Review. (C. O. Research, Interviewer) Retrieved from https://www.youtube.com/watch?v=NiDHOr3NHRA

27. Rowley, J. (2002). Using case studies in research. *Management Research News, 25*(1), 16-27. doi:https://doi.org/10.1108/01409170210782990 *scaling.* (n.d.). Retrieved from psc.dss.ucdavis.edu: psc.dss.ucdavis. edu

28. Sekaran, U. (2003). *Business Research Methods: A Skill Building Approach.* USA: John Wiley & Sons.

29. Support.minitab. (2017). *what-are-categorical-discrete-and-continuous-variables.* Retrieved from https://support.minitab.com: https://support.minitab.com/en-us/minitab-express/1/help-and-how-to/modeling-statistics/regression/supporting-topics/basics/what-are-categorical-discrete-and-continuous-variables/

30. UGC. (2018, July 23). *Notices.* Retrieved from www.ugc.ac.in: https://www.ugc.ac.in/pdfnews/7771545_academic-integrity-Regulation2018.pdf

31. Verma, K. A. (2013). *market-research-types.* Retrieved from http://whatismarketresearch.com: http://whatismarketresearch.com/market-research-types/what-is-syndicated-research/

32. Weiers, R. M. (2008). *Introduction to Business Research .* USA: Thomson SW .

33. Wilson, J. (2014). *Essentials of Business Research.* New Delhi: Sage.

34. www.statmethods.net. (n.d.). *Discriminant Function Analysis.* Retrieved from www.statmethods.net: https://www.statmethods.net/advstats/discriminant.html

35. www.surveymonkey.com. (2019). *how-to-use-an-interval-scale-in-your-survey-questions*. Retrieved from www.surveymonkey.com: https://www.surveymonkey.com/mp/how-to-use-an-interval-scale-in-your-survey-questions/
36. *www.syndicateresearch.com*. (2018). Retrieved from https://www.syndicateresearch.com/.
37. Zikmund, W. G., Babin, B. J., & Carr, J. C. (2009). *Business research methods:8th ed.* OH: South-Western College Pub.

References

1.1 Random Number Table

TABLE 1 - RANDOM DIGITS

11164	36318	75061	37674	26320	75100	10431	20418	19228	91792
21215	91791	76831	58678	87054	31687	93205	43685	19732	08468
10438	44482	66558	37649	08882	90870	12462	41810	01806	02977
36792	26236	33266	66583	60881	97395	20461	36742	02852	50564
73944	04773	12032	51414	82384	38370	00249	80709	72605	67497
49563	12872	14063	93104	78483	72717	68714	18048	25005	04151
64208	48237	41701	73117	33242	42314	83049	21933	92813	04763
51486	72875	38605	29341	80749	80151	33835	52602	79147	08868
99756	26360	64516	17971	48478	09610	04638	17141	09227	10606
71325	55217	13015	72907	00431	45117	33827	92873	02953	85474
65285	97198	12138	53010	94601	15838	16805	61004	43516	17020
17264	57327	38224	29301	31381	38109	34976	65692	98566	29550
95639	99754	31199	92558	68368	04985	51092	37780	40261	14479
61555	76404	86210	11808	12841	45147	97438	60022	12645	62000
78137	98768	04689	87130	79225	08153	84967	64539	79493	74917
62490	99215	84987	28759	19177	14733	24550	28067	68894	38490
24216	63444	21283	07044	92729	37284	13211	37485	10415	36457
16975	95428	33226	55903	31605	43817	22250	03918	46999	98501
59138	39542	71168	57609	91510	77904	74244	50940	31553	62562
29478	59652	50414	31966	87912	87154	12944	49862	96566	48825
96155	95009	27429	72918	08457	78134	48407	26061	58754	05326
29621	66583	62966	12468	20245	14015	04014	35713	03980	03024
12639	75291	71020	17265	41598	64074	64629	63293	53307	48766
14544	37134	54714	02401	63228	26831	19386	15457	17999	18306
83403	88827	09834	11333	68431	31706	26652	04711	34593	22561
67642	05204	30697	44806	96989	68403	85621	45556	35434	09532
64041	99011	14610	40273	09482	62864	01573	82274	81446	32477
17048	94523	97444	59904	16936	39384	97551	09620	63932	03091
93039	89416	52795	10631	09728	68202	20963	02477	55494	39563
82244	34392	96607	17220	51984	10753	76272	50985	97593	34320
96990	55244	70693	25255	40029	23289	48819	07159	60172	81697
09119	74803	97303	88701	51380	73143	98251	78635	27556	20712
57666	41204	47589	78364	38266	94393	70713	53388	79865	92069
46492	61594	26729	58272	81754	14648	77210	12923	53712	87771
08433	19172	08320	20839	13715	10597	17234	39355	74816	03363
10011	75004	86054	41190	10061	19660	03500	68412	57812	57929
92420	65431	16530	05547	10683	88102	30176	84750	10115	69220
35542	55865	07304	47010	43233	57022	52161	82976	47981	46588
86595	26247	18552	29491	33712	32285	64844	69395	41387	87195
72115	34985	58036	99137	47482	06204	24138	24272	16196	04393
07428	58863	96023	88936	51343	70958	96768	74317	27176	29600
35379	27922	28906	55013	26937	48174	04197	36074	65315	12537
10982	22807	10920	26299	23593	64629	57801	10437	43965	15344
90127	33341	77806	12446	15444	49244	47277	11346	15884	28131
63002	12990	23510	68774	48983	20481	59815	67248	17076	78910
40779	86382	48454	65269	91239	45989	45389	54847	77919	41105
43216	12608	18167	84631	94058	82458	15139	76856	86019	47928
96167	64375	74108	93643	09204	98855	59051	56492	11933	64958
70975	62693	35684	72607	23026	37004	32989	24843	01128	74658
85812	61875	23570	75754	29090	40264	80399	47254	40135	69916

TABLE 2 – RANDOM DIGITS

40603	16152	83235	37361	98783	24838	39793	80954	76865	32713
40941	53585	69958	60916	71018	90561	84505	53980	64735	85140
73505	83472	55953	17957	11446	22618	34771	25777	27064	13526
39412	16013	11442	89320	11307	49396	39805	12249	57656	88686
57994	76748	54627	48511	78646	33287	35524	54522	08795	56273
61834	59199	15469	82285	84164	91333	90954	87186	31598	25942
91402	77227	79516	21007	58602	81418	87838	18443	76162	51146
58299	83880	20125	10794	37780	61705	18276	99041	78135	99661
40684	99948	33880	76413	63839	71371	32392	51812	48248	96419
75978	64298	08074	62055	73864	01926	78374	15741	74452	49954
34556	39861	88267	76068	62445	64361	78685	24246	27027	48239
65990	57048	25067	77571	77974	37634	81564	98608	37224	49848
16381	15069	25416	87875	90374	86203	29677	82543	37554	89179
52458	88880	78352	67913	09245	47773	51272	06976	99571	33365
33007	85607	92008	44897	24964	50559	79549	85658	96865	24186
38712	31512	08588	61490	72294	42862	87334	05866	66269	43158
58722	03678	19186	69602	34625	75958	56869	17907	81867	11535
26188	69497	51351	47799	20477	71786	52560	66827	79419	70886
12893	54048	07255	86149	99090	70958	50775	31768	52903	27645
33186	81346	85095	37282	85536	72661	32180	40229	19209	74939
79893	29448	88392	54211	61708	83452	61227	81690	42265	20310
48449	15102	44126	19438	23382	14985	37538	30120	82443	11152
94205	04259	68983	50561	06902	10269	22216	70210	60736	58772
38648	09278	81313	77400	41126	52614	93613	27263	99381	49500
04292	46028	75666	26954	34979	68381	45154	09314	81009	05114
17026	49737	85875	12139	59391	81830	30185	83095	78752	40899
48070	76848	02531	97737	10151	18169	31709	74842	85522	74092
30159	95450	83778	46115	99178	97718	98440	15076	21199	20492
12148	92231	31361	60650	54695	30035	22765	91386	70399	79270
73838	77067	24863	97576	01139	54219	02959	45696	98103	78867
73547	43759	95632	39555	74391	07579	69491	02647	17050	49869
07277	93217	79421	21769	83572	48019	17327	99638	87035	89300
65128	48334	07493	28098	52087	55519	83718	60904	48721	17522
38716	61380	60212	05099	21210	22052	01780	36813	19528	07727
31921	76458	73720	08657	74922	61335	41690	41967	50691	30508
57238	27464	61487	52329	26150	79991	64398	91273	26824	94827
24219	41090	08531	61578	08236	41140	76335	91189	66312	44000
31309	49387	02330	02476	96074	33256	48554	95401	02642	29119
20750	97024	72619	66628	66509	31206	55293	24249	02266	39010
28537	84395	26654	37851	80590	53446	34385	86893	87713	26842
97929	41220	86431	94485	28778	44997	38802	56594	61363	04206
40568	33222	40486	91122	43294	94541	40988	02929	83190	74247
41483	92935	17061	78252	40498	43164	68646	33023	64333	64083
93040	66476	24990	41099	65135	37641	97613	87282	63693	55299
76869	39300	84978	07504	36835	72748	47644	48542	25076	68626
02982	57991	50765	91930	21375	35604	29963	13738	03155	59914
94479	76500	39170	06629	10031	48724	49822	44021	44335	26474
52291	75822	95966	90947	65031	75913	52654	63377	70664	60082
03684	03600	52831	55381	97013	19993	41295	29118	18710	64851
58939	28366	86765	67465	45421	74228	01095	50987	83833	37216

References

135

TABLE 3 – RANDOM DIGITS

37100	62492	63642	47638	13925	80113	88067	42575	44078	62703
53406	13855	38519	29500	62479	01036	87964	44498	07793	21599
55172	81556	18856	59043	64315	38270	25677	01965	21310	28115
40353	84807	47767	46890	16053	32415	60259	99788	55924	22077
18899	09612	77541	57675	70153	41179	97535	82889	27214	03482
68141	25340	92551	11326	60939	79355	41544	88926	09111	86431
51559	91159	81310	63251	91799	41215	87412	35317	74271	11603
92214	33386	73459	79359	65867	39269	57527	69551	17495	91456
15089	50557	33166	87094	52425	21211	41876	42525	36625	63964
96461	00604	11120	22254	16763	19206	67790	88362	01880	37911
28177	44111	15705	73835	69399	33602	13660	84342	97667	80847
66953	44737	81127	07493	07861	12666	85077	95972	96556	80108
19712	27263	84575	49820	19837	69985	34931	67935	71903	82560
68756	64757	19987	92222	11691	42502	00952	47981	97579	93408
75022	65332	98606	29451	57349	39219	08585	31502	96936	96356
11323	70069	90269	89266	46413	61615	66447	49751	15836	97343
55208	63470	18158	25283	19335	53893	87746	72531	16826	52605
11474	08786	05594	67045	13231	51186	71500	50498	59487	48677
81422	86842	60997	79669	43804	78690	58358	87639	24427	66799
21771	75963	23151	90274	08275	50677	99384	94022	84888	80139
42278	12160	22576	14278	34231	20724	27908	02657	19023	07190
17697	60114	63247	32096	32503	04923	17570	73243	76181	99343
05686	30243	34124	02936	71749	03031	72259	26351	77511	00850
52992	46650	89910	57395	39502	49738	87854	71066	84596	33115
94518	93984	81478	67750	89354	01080	25988	84359	31088	13655
00184	72186	78906	75480	71140	15199	69002	08374	22126	23555
87462	63165	79816	61630	50140	95319	79205	79202	67414	60805
88692	58716	12273	48176	86038	78474	76730	82931	51595	20747
20094	42962	41382	16768	13261	13510	04822	96354	72001	68642
60935	81504	50520	82153	27892	18029	79663	44146	72876	67843
51392	85936	43898	50596	81121	98122	69196	54271	12059	62539
54239	41918	79526	46274	24853	67165	12011	04923	20273	89405
57892	73394	07160	90262	48731	46648	70977	58262	78359	50436
02330	74736	53274	44468	53616	35794	54838	39114	68302	26855
76115	29247	55342	51299	79908	36613	68361	18864	13419	34950
63312	81886	29085	20101	38037	34742	78364	39356	40006	49800
27632	21570	34274	56426	00330	07117	86673	46455	66866	76374
06335	62111	44014	52567	79480	45886	92585	87828	17376	35254
64142	87676	21358	88773	10604	62834	63971	03989	21421	76086
28436	25468	75235	75370	63543	76266	27745	31714	04219	00699
09522	83855	85973	15888	29554	17995	37443	11461	42909	32634
93714	15414	93712	02742	34395	21929	38928	31205	01838	60000
15681	53599	58185	73840	88758	10618	98725	23146	13521	47905
77712	23914	08907	43768	10304	61405	53986	61116	76164	54958
78453	54844	61509	01245	91199	07482	02534	08189	62978	55516
24860	68284	19367	29073	93464	06714	45268	60678	58506	23700
37284	06844	78887	57276	42695	03682	83240	09744	63025	60997
35488	52473	37634	32569	39590	27379	23520	29714	03743	08444
51595	59909	35223	44991	29830	56614	59661	83397	38421	17503
90660	35171	30021	91120	78793	16827	89320	08260	09181	53616

TABLE 4 – RANDOM DIGITS

54723	56527	53076	38235	42780	22716	36400	48028	78196	92985
84828	81248	25548	34075	43459	44628	21866	90350	82264	20478
65799	01914	81363	05173	23674	41774	25154	73003	87031	94368
87917	38549	48213	71708	92035	92527	55484	32274	87918	22455
26907	88173	71189	28377	13785	87469	35647	19695	33401	51998
68052	65422	88460	06352	42379	55499	60469	76931	83430	24560
42587	68149	88147	99700	56124	53239	38726	63652	36644	50876
97176	55416	67642	05051	89931	19482	80720	48977	70004	03664
53295	87133	38264	94708	00703	35991	76404	82249	22942	49659
23011	94108	29196	65187	69974	01970	31667	54307	40032	30031
75768	49549	24543	63285	32803	18301	80851	89301	02398	99891
86668	70341	66460	75648	78678	27770	30245	44775	56120	44235
56727	72036	50347	33521	05068	47248	67832	30960	95465	32217
27936	78010	09617	04408	18954	61862	64547	52453	83213	47833
31994	69072	37354	93025	38934	90219	91148	62757	51703	84040
02985	95303	15182	50166	11755	56256	89546	31170	87221	63267
89965	10206	95830	95406	33845	87588	70237	84360	19629	72568
45587	29611	98579	42481	05359	36578	56047	68114	58583	16313
01071	08530	74305	77509	16270	20889	99753	88035	55643	18291
90209	68521	14293	39194	68803	32052	39413	26883	83119	69623
04982	68470	27875	15480	13206	44784	83601	03172	07817	01520
19740	24637	97377	32112	74283	69384	49768	64141	02024	85380
50197	79869	86497	68709	42073	28498	82750	43571	77075	07123
46954	67536	28968	81936	95999	04319	09932	66223	45491	69503
82549	62676	31123	49899	70512	95288	15517	85352	21987	08669
61798	81600	80018	84742	06103	60786	01408	75967	29948	21454
57666	29055	46518	01487	30136	14349	56159	47408	78311	25896
29805	64994	66872	62230	41385	58066	96600	99301	85976	84194
06711	34939	19599	76247	87879	97114	74314	39599	43544	36255
13934	46885	58315	88366	06138	37923	11192	90757	10831	01580
28549	98327	99943	25377	17628	65468	07875	16728	22602	33892
40871	61803	25767	55484	90997	86941	64027	01020	39518	34693
47704	38355	71708	80117	11361	88875	22315	38048	42891	87885
62611	19698	09304	29265	07636	08508	23773	56545	08015	28891
03047	83981	11916	09267	67316	87952	27045	62536	32180	60936
26460	50501	31731	18938	11025	18515	31747	96828	58258	97107
01764	25959	69293	89875	72710	49659	66632	25314	95260	22146
11762	54806	02651	52912	32770	64507	59090	01275	47624	16124
31736	31695	11523	64213	91190	10145	34231	36405	65860	48771
97155	48706	52239	21831	49043	18650	72246	43729	63368	53822
31181	49672	17237	04024	65324	32460	01566	67342	94986	36106
32115	82683	67182	89030	41370	50266	19505	57724	93358	49445
07068	75947	71743	69285	30395	81818	36125	52055	20289	16911
26622	74184	75166	96748	34729	61289	36908	73686	84641	45130
02805	52676	22519	47848	68210	23954	63085	87729	14176	45410
32301	58701	04193	30142	99779	21697	05059	26684	63516	75925
26339	56909	39331	42101	01031	01947	02257	47236	19913	90371
95274	09508	81012	42413	11278	19354	68661	04192	36878	84366
24275	39632	09777	98800	48027	96908	08177	15364	02317	89548
36116	42128	65401	94199	51058	10759	47244	99830	64255	40516

References 137

TABLE 5 – RANDOM DIGITS

47505	02008	20300	87188	42505	40294	04404	59286	95914	07191
13350	08414	64049	94377	91059	74531	56228	12307	87871	97064
33006	92690	69248	97443	38841	05051	33756	24736	43508	53566
55216	63886	06804	11861	30968	74515	40112	40432	18682	02845
21991	26228	14801	19192	45110	39937	81966	23258	99348	61219
71025	28212	10474	27522	16356	78456	46814	28975	01014	91458
65522	15242	84554	74560	26206	49520	65702	54193	25583	54745
27975	54923	90650	06170	99006	75651	77622	20491	53329	12452
07300	09704	36099	61577	34632	55176	87366	19968	33986	46445
54357	13689	19569	03814	47873	34086	28474	05131	46619	41499
00977	04481	42044	08649	83107	02423	46919	59586	58337	32280
13920	78761	12311	92808	71581	85251	11417	85252	61312	10266
08395	37043	37880	34172	80411	05181	58091	41269	22626	64799
46166	67206	01619	43769	91727	06149	17924	42628	57647	76936
87767	77607	03742	01613	83528	66251	75822	83058	97584	45401
29880	95288	21644	46587	11576	30568	56687	83239	76388	17857
36248	36666	14894	59273	04518	11307	67655	08566	51759	41795
12386	29656	30474	25964	10006	86382	46680	93060	52337	56034
52068	73801	52188	19491	76221	45685	95189	78577	36250	36082
41727	52171	56719	06054	34898	93990	89263	79180	39917	16122
49319	74580	57470	14600	22224	49028	93024	21414	90150	15686
88786	76963	12127	23014	91393	98208	27991	12539	11357	69512
84866	95202	43983	72655	89684	79005	85932	41627	87381	38832
11849	26482	20461	99450	21636	13337	55407	01897	75422	05205
54966	17594	57393	73267	87106	26849	68667	45791	87226	74412
10959	33349	80719	96751	25752	17133	32786	34368	77600	41809
22784	07783	35903	00091	73954	48706	83423	96286	90373	23372
86037	61791	33815	63968	70437	33124	50025	44367	98637	40870
80037	65089	85919	74391	36170	82988	52311	59180	37846	98028
72751	84359	15769	13615	70866	37007	74565	92781	37770	76451
18532	03874	66220	79050	66814	76341	42452	65365	07167	90134
22936	22058	49171	11027	07066	14606	11759	19942	21909	15031
66397	76510	81150	00704	94990	68204	07242	82922	65745	51503
89730	23272	65420	35091	16227	87024	56662	59110	11158	67508
81821	75323	96068	91724	94679	88062	13729	94152	59343	07352
94377	82554	53586	11432	08788	74053	98312	61732	91248	23673
68485	49991	53165	19865	30288	00467	98105	91483	89389	61991
07330	07184	86788	64577	47692	45031	36325	47029	27914	24905
10993	14930	35072	36429	26176	66205	07758	07982	33721	81319
20801	15178	64453	83357	21589	23153	60375	63305	37995	66275
79241	35347	66851	79247	57462	23893	16542	55775	06813	63512
43593	39555	97345	58494	52892	55080	19056	96192	61508	23165
29522	62713	33701	17186	15721	95018	76571	58615	35836	66260
88836	47290	67274	78362	84457	39181	17295	39626	82373	10883
65905	66253	91482	30689	81313	01343	37188	37756	04182	19376
44798	69371	07865	91756	42318	63601	53872	93610	44142	89830
35510	99139	32031	27925	03560	33806	85092	70436	94777	57963
50125	93223	64209	49714	73379	89975	38567	44316	60262	10777
25173	90038	63871	40418	23818	63250	05118	52700	92327	55449
68459	90094	44995	93718	83654	79311	18107	12557	09179	28416

TABLE 6 – RANDOM DIGITS

96195	07059	13266	31389	87612	88004	31843	83469	22793	14312
22408	94958	19095	58035	43831	32354	83946	57964	70404	32017
53896	23508	16227	56929	74329	12264	26047	66844	47383	42202
22565	02475	00258	79018	70090	37914	27755	00872	71553	56684
49438	20772	60846	69732	07612	70474	46483	21053	95475	53448
65620	34684	00210	04863	01373	19978	61682	69315	46766	83768
20246	26941	41298	04763	19769	25865	95937	03545	93561	73871
09433	09167	35166	32731	73299	41137	37328	28301	61629	05040
95552	73456	16578	88140	80059	50296	07656	01396	83099	09718
76053	05150	69125	69442	16509	03495	26427	58780	27576	31342
34822	35843	78468	82380	52313	71070	71273	10768	86101	51474
07753	04073	58520	80022	28185	16432	86909	82347	10548	83929
04204	94434	62798	81902	29977	57258	87826	35003	46449	76636
96770	19440	29700	42093	64369	69176	29732	37389	34054	28680
65989	62843	10917	34458	81936	84775	39415	10622	36102	16753
06644	94784	66995	61812	54215	01336	75887	57685	66114	76984
88950	46077	34651	12038	87914	20785	39705	73898	12318	78334
21482	95422	02002	33671	46764	50527	46276	77570	68457	62199
55137	61039	02006	69913	11291	87215	89991	26003	55271	08153
98441	81529	59607	65225	49051	28328	85535	37003	87211	10204
57168	30458	23892	07825	53447	53511	09315	42552	43135	57892
71886	65334	38013	09379	83976	42441	14086	33197	82671	05037
40418	59504	52383	07232	14179	59693	37668	26689	93865	78925
28833	76661	47277	92935	63193	94862	60560	72484	29755	40894
37883	62124	62199	49542	55083	20575	44636	92282	52105	77664
44882	33592	66234	13821	86342	00135	87938	57995	34157	99858
19082	13873	07184	21566	95320	28968	31911	06288	77271	76171
45316	29283	89318	55806	89338	79231	91545	55477	19552	03471
22788	55433	31188	74882	44858	69655	08096	70982	61300	23792
08293	86193	05026	21255	63082	92946	28748	25423	45282	57821
29223	70541	67115	84584	10100	33854	26466	77796	70698	99393
22681	80110	31595	09246	39147	11158	43298	36220	88841	11271
74580	90354	43744	22178	38084	60027	24201	71686	59767	33274
69093	71364	08107	96952	50005	30297	97417	89575	04676	35616
40456	91234	58090	65342	95002	28447	21'700	43137	13746	85959
72927	67349	83962	58912	59734	76323	02913	46306	53956	38936
61869	33093	81129	06481	89281	83629	81960	63704	56329	10357
40048	16520	07638	10797	22270	57350	72214	36410	95526	87614
68773	97669	28656	89938	12917	25630	08068	19445	76250	24727
09774	30751	49740	11385	91468	28900	76804	52460	52320	70493
46139	36689	82587	13586	35061	76128	38568	62300	43439	53434
26566	95323	32993	89988	12152	01862	93113	33875	31730	62941
06765	57141	48617	18282	13086	76064	83334	70192	15972	80429
35384	90380	12317	89702	33091	68835	62960	38010	52710	87604
49333	78482	36199	11355	86044	88760	03724	22927	91716	92332
45595	14044	56806	99126	85584	87750	78149	22723	48245	78126
79819	15054	76174	12206	06886	06814	43285	20008	75345	19779
11971	62234	74857	46401	20817	57591	41189	49604	29604	30660
11452	89318	53084	21993	62471	74101	61217	76536	58393	63718
38746	81271	96260	98137	60275	22647	33103	50090	29395	10016

References 139

TABLE 7 – RANDOM DIGITS

93369	13044	69686	78162	29132	51544	17925	56738	32683	83153
19360	55049	94951	76341	38159	31008	41476	05278	03909	02299
47798	89890	06893	65483	97658	74884	38611	27264	26956	83504
69223	32007	03513	61149	66270	73087	16795	76845	44645	44552
34511	50721	84850	34159	38985	75384	22965	55366	81632	78872
54031	59329	58963	52220	76806	98715	67452	78741	58128	00077
66722	85515	04723	92411	03834	12109	85185	37350	93614	15351
71059	07496	38404	18126	37894	44991	45777	02070	38159	23930
45478	86066	31135	33243	01190	47277	55146	56130	70117	83203
97246	91121	89437	20393	76598	99458	76665	83793	37448	32664
22982	25936	96417	34845	28942	65569	38253	77182	12996	19505
48243	62993	47132	85248	79160	90981	71696	79609	33809	60839
93514	14915	67960	82203	22598	94802	75332	95585	69542	79924
69707	98303	93069	16216	01542	51771	16833	20922	94415	27617
87467	91794	70814	12743	17543	04057	71231	11309	32780	83270
81006	81498	59375	30502	44868	81279	23585	49678	70014	10523
15458	83481	50187	43375	56644	72076	59403	65469	74760	69509
33469	12510	23095	48016	22064	39774	07373	10555	33345	21787
67198	07176	65996	18317	83083	11921	06254	68437	59481	54778
58037	92261	85504	55690	63488	26451	43223	38009	50567	09191
84983	68312	25519	56158	22390	12823	92390	28947	36708	25393
35554	02935	72889	68112	19114	14336	50716	63003	86391	94074
04368	17632	50962	71908	13105	76285	31819	16884	11665	16594
81311	60479	69985	30952	93067	70056	55229	83226	22555	66447
03823	89887	55828	74452	21692	55847	15960	47521	27784	25728
80422	65437	38797	56261	88300	35980	56656	45662	29219	49257
61307	49468	43344	43700	14074	19739	03275	99444	62545	23720
83873	82557	10002	80093	74645	33109	15281	38759	09342	69408
38110	16855	28922	93758	22885	36706	92542	60270	99599	17983
43892	91189	87226	56935	99836	85489	89693	49475	31941	78065
93683	09664	53927	49885	94979	88848	42642	93218	80305	49428
32748	02121	11972	96914	83264	89016	45140	20362	63242	86255
49211	92963	38625	65312	52156	36400	67050	64058	45489	24165
63365	64224	69475	57512	85097	05054	88673	96593	00902	53320
63576	26373	44610	43748	90399	06770	71609	90916	69002	57180
41078	47036	65524	68466	77613	20076	71969	47706	22506	81053
70846	89558	64173	15381	67322	70097	82363	90767	17879	32697
68800	64492	20162	32707	69510	82465	26821	79917	34615	35820
44977	89525	51269	63747	30997	97213	53016	65909	05723	50168
79354	63847	24395	53679	07667	67993	24634	78867	78516	00448
14954	22299	40156	52685	19093	06090	23800	06739	76836	19050
01711	98439	09446	33937	98956	85676	89493	05132	45886	49379
62328	55328	45738	93940	15772	81975	91017	21387	57949	13992
73004	62109	81907	71077	50322	66093	79921	61412	18347	21115
34218	89445	03609	52336	19005	15179	94958	99448	11612	76981
99159	01968	45886	86875	05196	64297	59339	39878	61548	56442
92858	29949	15817	93372	34732	61584	72007	58597	43802	51066
27396	97477	65554	71601	01540	26509	19487	39684	18676	41219
37103	45309	30129	43380	66638	10841	77292	40288	25826	61431
57347	97012	48428	20606	54138	75716	23741	50462	13221	47216

2.1 Standardized Normal Distribution

STANDARD NORMAL DISTRIBUTION: Table Values Represent AREA to the LEFT of the Z score.									
Z	.00	.01	.02	.03	.04	.05	.06	.07	.08	.09
-3.9	.00005	.00005	.00004	.00004	.00004	.00004	.00004	.00004	.00003	.00003
-3.8	.00007	.00007	.00007	.00006	.00006	.00006	.00006	.00005	.00005	.00005
-3.7	.00011	.00010	.00010	.00010	.00009	.00009	.00008	.00008	.00008	.00008
-3.6	.00016	.00015	.00015	.00014	.00014	.00013	.00013	.00012	.00012	.00011
-3.5	.00023	.00022	.00022	.00021	.00020	.00019	.00019	.00018	.00017	.00017
-3.4	.00034	.00032	.00031	.00030	.00029	.00028	.00027	.00026	.00025	.00024
-3.3	.00048	.00047	.00045	.00043	.00042	.00040	.00039	.00038	.00036	.00035
-3.2	.00069	.00066	.00064	.00062	.00060	.00058	.00056	.00054	.00052	.00050
-3.1	.00097	.00094	.00090	.00087	.00084	.00082	.00079	.00076	.00074	.00071
-3.0	.00135	.00131	.00126	.00122	.00118	.00114	.00111	.00107	.00104	.00100
-2.9	.00187	.00181	.00175	.00169	.00164	.00159	.00154	.00149	.00144	.00139
-2.8	.00256	.00248	.00240	.00233	.00226	.00219	.00212	.00205	.00199	.00193
-2.7	.00347	.00336	.00326	.00317	.00307	.00298	.00289	.00280	.00272	.00264
-2.6	.00466	.00453	.00440	.00427	.00415	.00402	.00391	.00379	.00368	.00357
-2.5	.00621	.00604	.00587	.00570	.00554	.00539	.00523	.00508	.00494	.00480
-2.4	.00820	.00798	.00776	.00755	.00734	.00714	.00695	.00676	.00657	.00639
-2.3	.01072	.01044	.01017	.00990	.00964	.00939	.00914	.00889	.00866	.00842
-2.2	.01390	.01355	.01321	.01287	.01255	.01222	.01191	.01160	.01130	.01101
-2.1	.01786	.01743	.01700	.01659	.01618	.01578	.01539	.01500	.01463	.01426
-2.0	.02275	.02222	.02169	.02118	.02068	.02018	.01970	.01923	.01876	.01831
-1.9	.02872	.02807	.02743	.02680	.02619	.02559	.02500	.02442	.02385	.02330
-1.8	.03593	.03515	.03438	.03362	.03288	.03216	.03144	.03074	.03005	.02938
-1.7	.04457	.04363	.04272	.04182	.04093	.04006	.03920	.03836	.03754	.03673
-1.6	.05480	.05370	.05262	.05155	.05050	.04947	.04846	.04746	.04648	.04551
-1.5	.06681	.06552	.06426	.06301	.06178	.06057	.05938	.05821	.05705	.05592
-1.4	.08076	.07927	.07780	.07636	.07493	.07353	.07215	.07078	.06944	.06811
-1.3	.09680	.09510	.09342	.09176	.09012	.08851	.08691	.08534	.08379	.08226
-1.2	.11507	.11314	.11123	.10935	.10749	.10565	.10383	.10204	.10027	.09853
-1.1	.13567	.13350	.13136	.12924	.12714	.12507	.12302	.12100	.11900	.11702
-1.0	.15866	.15625	.15386	.15151	.14917	.14686	.14457	.14231	.14007	.13786
-0.9	.18406	.18141	.17879	.17619	.17361	.17106	.16853	.16602	.16354	.16109
-0.8	.21186	.20897	.20611	.20327	.20045	.19766	.19489	.19215	.18943	.18673
-0.7	.24196	.23885	.23576	.23270	.22965	.22663	.22363	.22065	.21770	.21476
-0.6	.27425	.27093	.26763	.26435	.26109	.25785	.25463	.25143	.24825	.24510
-0.5	.30854	.30503	.30153	.29806	.29460	.29116	.28774	.28434	.28096	.27760
-0.4	.34458	.34090	.33724	.33360	.32997	.32636	.32276	.31918	.31561	.31207
-0.3	.38209	.37828	.37448	.37070	.36693	.36317	.35942	.35569	.35197	.34827
-0.2	.42074	.41683	.41294	.40905	.40517	.40129	.39743	.39358	.38974	.38591
-0.1	.46017	.45620	.45224	.44828	.44433	.44038	.43644	.43251	.42858	.42465
-0.0	.50000	.49601	.49202	.48803	.48405	.48006	.47608	.47210	.46812	.46414

Contd...

References 141

2.1 Standardized Normal Distribution *(Contd...)*

STANDARD NORMAL DISTRIBUTION: Table Values Represent AREA to the LEFT of the Z score.

Z	.00	.01	.02	.03	.04	.05	.06	.07	.08	.09
0.0	.50000	.50399	.50798	.51197	.51595	.51994	.52392	.52790	.53188	.53586
0.1	.53983	.54380	.54776	.55172	.55567	.55962	.56356	.56749	.57142	.57535
0.2	.57926	.58317	.58706	.59095	.59483	.59871	.60257	.60642	.61026	.61409
0.3	.61791	.62172	.62552	.62930	.63307	.63683	.64058	.64431	.64803	.65173
0.4	.65542	.65910	.66276	.66640	.67003	.67364	.67724	.68082	.68439	.68793
0.5	.69146	.69497	.69847	.70194	.70540	.70884	.71226	.71566	.71904	.72240
0.6	.72575	.72907	.73237	.73565	.73891	.74215	.74537	.74857	.75175	.75490
0.7	.75804	.76115	.76424	.76730	.77035	.77337	.77637	.77935	.78230	.78524
0.8	.78814	.79103	.79389	.79673	.79955	.80234	.80511	.80785	.81057	.81327
0.9	.81594	.81859	.82121	.82381	.82639	.82894	.83147	.83398	.83646	.83891
1.0	.84134	.84375	.84614	.84849	.85083	.85314	.85543	.85769	.85993	.86214
1.1	.86433	.86650	.86864	.87076	.87286	.87493	.87698	.87900	.88100	.88298
1.2	.88493	.88686	.88877	.89065	.89251	.89435	.89617	.89796	.89973	.90147
1.3	.90320	.90490	.90658	.90824	.90988	.91149	.91309	.91466	.91621	.91774
1.4	.91924	.92073	.92220	.92364	.92507	.92647	.92785	.92922	.93056	.93189
1.5	.93319	.93448	.93574	.93699	.93822	.93943	.94062	.94179	.94295	.94408
1.6	.94520	.94630	.94738	.94845	.94950	.95053	.95154	.95254	.95352	.95449
1.7	.95543	.95637	.95728	.95818	.95907	.95994	.96080	.96164	.96246	.96327
1.8	.96407	.96485	.96562	.96638	.96712	.96784	.96856	.96926	.96995	.97062
1.9	.97128	.97193	.97257	.97320	.97381	.97441	.97500	.97558	.97615	.97670
2.0	.97725	.97778	.97831	.97882	.97932	.97982	.98030	.98077	.98124	.98169
2.1	.98214	.98257	.98300	.98341	.98382	.98422	.98461	.98500	.98537	.98574
2.2	.98610	.98645	.98679	.98713	.98745	.98778	.98809	.98840	.98870	.98899
2.3	.98928	.98956	.98983	.99010	.99036	.99061	.99086	.99111	.99134	.99158
2.4	.99180	.99202	.99224	.99245	.99266	.99286	.99305	.99324	.99343	.99361
2.5	.99379	.99396	.99413	.99430	.99446	.99461	.99477	.99492	.99506	.99520
2.6	.99534	.99547	.99560	.99573	.99585	.99598	.99609	.99621	.99632	.99643
2.7	.99653	.99664	.99674	.99683	.99693	.99702	.99711	.99720	.99728	.99736
2.8	.99744	.99752	.99760	.99767	.99774	.99781	.99788	.99795	.99801	.99807
2.9	.99813	.99819	.99825	.99831	.99836	.99841	.99846	.99851	.99856	.99861
3.0	.99865	.99869	.99874	.99878	.99882	.99886	.99889	.99893	.99896	.99900
3.1	.99903	.99906	.99910	.99913	.99916	.99918	.99921	.99924	.99926	.99929
3.2	.99931	.99934	.99936	.99938	.99940	.99942	.99944	.99946	.99948	.99950
3.3	.99952	.99953	.99955	.99957	.99958	.99960	.99961	.99962	.99964	.99965
3.4	.99966	.99968	.99969	.99970	.99971	.99972	.99973	.99974	.99975	.99976
3.5	.99977	.99978	.99978	.99979	.99980	.99981	.99981	.99982	.99983	.99983
3.6	.99984	.99985	.99985	.99986	.99986	.99987	.99987	.99988	.99988	.99989
3.7	.99989	.99990	.99990	.99990	.99991	.99991	.99992	.99992	.99992	.99992
3.8	.99993	.99993	.99993	.99994	.99994	.99994	.99994	.99995	.99995	.99995
3.9	.99995	.99995	.99996	.99996	.99996	.99996	.99996	.99996	.99997	.99997

3.1 Critical Value of t

t Table

cum. prob	$t_{.50}$	$t_{.75}$	$t_{.80}$	$t_{.85}$	$t_{.90}$	$t_{.95}$	$t_{.975}$	$t_{.99}$	$t_{.995}$	$t_{.999}$	$t_{.9995}$
one-tail	0.50	0.25	0.20	0.15	0.10	0.05	0.025	0.01	0.005	0.001	0.0005
two-tails	1.00	0.50	0.40	0.30	0.20	0.10	0.05	0.02	0.01	0.002	0.001
df											
1	0.000	1.000	1.376	1.963	3.078	6.314	12.71	31.82	63.66	318.31	636.62
2	0.000	0.816	1.061	1.386	1.886	2.920	4.303	6.965	9.925	22.327	31.599
3	0.000	0.765	0.978	1.250	1.638	2.353	3.182	4.541	5.841	10.215	12.924
4	0.000	0.741	0.941	1.190	1.533	2.132	2.776	3.747	4.604	7.173	8.610
5	0.000	0.727	0.920	1.156	1.476	2.015	2.571	3.365	4.032	5.893	6.869
6	0.000	0.718	0.906	1.134	1.440	1.943	2.447	3.143	3.707	5.208	5.959
7	0.000	0.711	0.896	1.119	1.415	1.895	2.365	2.998	3.499	4.785	5.408
8	0.000	0.706	0.889	1.108	1.397	1.860	2.306	2.896	3.355	4.501	5.041
9	0.000	0.703	0.883	1.100	1.383	1.833	2.262	2.821	3.250	4.297	4.781
10	0.000	0.700	0.879	1.093	1.372	1.812	2.228	2.764	3.169	4.144	4.587
11	0.000	0.697	0.876	1.088	1.363	1.796	2.201	2.718	3.106	4.025	4.437
12	0.000	0.695	0.873	1.083	1.356	1.782	2.179	2.681	3.055	3.930	4.318
13	0.000	0.694	0.870	1.079	1.350	1.771	2.160	2.650	3.012	3.852	4.221
14	0.000	0.692	0.868	1.076	1.345	1.761	2.145	2.624	2.977	3.787	4.140
15	0.000	0.691	0.866	1.074	1.341	1.753	2.131	2.602	2.947	3.733	4.073
16	0.000	0.690	0.865	1.071	1.337	1.746	2.120	2.583	2.921	3.686	4.015
17	0.000	0.689	0.863	1.069	1.333	1.740	2.110	2.567	2.898	3.646	3.965
18	0.000	0.688	0.862	1.067	1.330	1.734	2.101	2.552	2.878	3.610	3.922
19	0.000	0.688	0.861	1.066	1.328	1.729	2.093	2.539	2.861	3.579	3.883
20	0.000	0.687	0.860	1.064	1.325	1.725	2.086	2.528	2.845	3.552	3.850
21	0.000	0.686	0.859	1.063	1.323	1.721	2.080	2.518	2.831	3.527	3.819
22	0.000	0.686	0.858	1.061	1.321	1.717	2.074	2.508	2.819	3.505	3.792
23	0.000	0.685	0.858	1.060	1.319	1.714	2.069	2.500	2.807	3.485	3.768
24	0.000	0.685	0.857	1.059	1.318	1.711	2.064	2.492	2.797	3.467	3.745
25	0.000	0.684	0.856	1.058	1.316	1.708	2.060	2.485	2.787	3.450	3.725
26	0.000	0.684	0.856	1.058	1.315	1.706	2.056	2.479	2.779	3.435	3.707
27	0.000	0.684	0.855	1.057	1.314	1.703	2.052	2.473	2.771	3.421	3.690
28	0.000	0.683	0.855	1.056	1.313	1.701	2.048	2.467	2.763	3.408	3.674
29	0.000	0.683	0.854	1.055	1.311	1.699	2.045	2.462	2.756	3.396	3.659
30	0.000	0.683	0.854	1.055	1.310	1.697	2.042	2.457	2.750	3.385	3.646
40	0.000	0.681	0.851	1.050	1.303	1.684	2.021	2.423	2.704	3.307	3.551
60	0.000	0.679	0.848	1.045	1.296	1.671	2.000	2.390	2.660	3.232	3.460
80	0.000	0.678	0.846	1.043	1.292	1.664	1.990	2.374	2.639	3.195	3.416
100	0.000	0.677	0.845	1.042	1.290	1.660	1.984	2.364	2.626	3.174	3.390
1000	0.000	0.675	0.842	1.037	1.282	1.646	1.962	2.330	2.581	3.098	3.300
z	0.000	0.674	0.842	1.036	1.282	1.645	1.960	2.326	2.576	3.090	3.291
	0%	50%	60%	70%	80%	90%	95%	98%	99%	99.8%	99.9%
						Confidence Level					

References

4.1 Critical Value of Chi-Square (χ^2)

Chi-square Distribution Table

d.f.	.995	.99	.975	.95	.9	.1	.05	.025	.01
1	0.00	0.00	0.00	0.00	0.02	2.71	3.84	5.02	6.63
2	0.01	0.02	0.05	0.10	0.21	4.61	5.99	7.38	9.21
3	0.07	0.11	0.22	0.35	0.58	6.25	7.81	9.35	11.34
4	0.21	0.30	0.48	0.71	1.06	7.78	9.49	11.14	13.28
5	0.41	0.55	0.83	1.15	1.61	9.24	11.07	12.83	15.09
6	0.68	0.87	1.24	1.64	2.20	10.64	12.59	14.45	16.81
7	0.99	1.24	1.69	2.17	2.83	12.02	14.07	16.01	18.48
8	1.34	1.65	2.18	2.73	3.49	13.36	15.51	17.53	20.09
9	1.73	2.09	2.70	3.33	4.17	14.68	16.92	19.02	21.67
10	2.16	2.56	3.25	3.94	4.87	15.99	18.31	20.48	23.21
11	2.60	3.05	3.82	4.57	5.58	17.28	19.68	21.92	24.72
12	3.07	3.57	4.40	5.23	6.30	18.55	21.03	23.34	26.22
13	3.57	4.11	5.01	5.89	7.04	19.81	22.36	24.74	27.69
14	4.07	4.66	5.63	6.57	7.79	21.06	23.68	26.12	29.14
15	4.60	5.23	6.26	7.26	8.55	22.31	25.00	27.49	30.58
16	5.14	5.81	6.91	7.96	9.31	23.54	26.30	28.85	32.00
17	5.70	6.41	7.56	8.67	10.09	24.77	27.59	30.10	33.41
18	6.26	7.01	8.23	9.39	10.86	25.99	28.87	31.53	34.81
19	6.84	7.63	8.91	10.12	11.65	27.20	30.14	32.85	36.19
20	7.43	8.26	9.59	10.85	12.44	28.41	31.41	34.17	37.57
22	8.64	9.54	10.98	12.34	14.04	30.81	33.92	36.78	40.29
24	9.89	10.86	12.40	13.85	15.66	33.20	36.42	39.36	42.98
26	11.16	12.20	13.84	15.38	17.29	35.56	38.89	41.92	45.64
28	12.46	13.56	15.31	16.93	18.94	37.92	41.34	44.46	48.28
30	13.79	14.95	16.79	18.49	20.60	40.26	43.77	46.98	50.89
32	15.13	16.36	18.29	20.07	22.27	42.58	46.19	49.48	53.49
34	16.50	17.79	19.81	21.66	23.95	44.90	48.60	51.97	56.06
38	19.29	20.69	22.88	24.88	27.34	49.51	53.38	56.90	61.16
42	22.14	23.65	26.00	28.14	30.77	54.09	58.12	61.78	66.21
46	25.04	26.66	29.16	31.44	34.22	58.64	62.83	66.62	71.20
50	27.99	29.71	32.36	34.76	37.69	63.17	67.50	71.42	76.15
55	31.73	33.57	36.40	38.96	42.06	68.80	73.31	77.38	82.29
60	35.53	37.48	40.48	43.19	46.46	74.40	79.08	83.30	88.38
65	39.38	41.44	44.60	47.45	50.88	79.97	84.82	89.18	94.42
70	43.28	45.44	48.76	51.74	55.33	85.53	90.53	95.02	100.43
75	47.21	49.48	52.94	56.05	59.79	91.06	96.22	100.84	106.39
80	51.17	53.54	57.15	60.39	64.28	96.58	101.88	106.63	112.33
85	55.17	57.63	61.39	64.75	68.78	102.08	107.52	112.39	118.24
90	59.20	61.75	65.65	69.13	73.29	107.57	113.15	118.14	124.12
95	63.25	65.90	69.92	73.52	77.82	113.04	118.75	123.86	129.97
100	67.33	70.06	74.22	77.93	82.36	118.50	124.34	129.56	135.81

5.1 Critical Value of F

Table of critical values for the F distribution (for use with ANOVA):

How to use this table:
There are two tables here. The first one gives critical values of F at the $p = 0.05$ level of significance. The second table gives critical values of F at the $p = 0.01$ level of significance.
1. Obtain your F-ratio. This has (x,y) degrees of freedom associated with it.
2. Go along x columns, and down y rows. The point of intersection is your critical F-ratio.
3. If your obtained value of F is equal to or larger than this critical F-value, then your result is significant at that level of probability.
An example: I obtain an F ratio of 3.96 with (2, 24) degrees of freedom.
I go along 2 columns and down 24 rows. The critical value of F is 3.40. My obtained F-ratio is larger than this, and so I conclude that my obtained F-ratio is likely to occur by chance with a $p<.05$.

Critical values of F for the 0.05 significance level:

	1	2	3	4	5	6	7	8	9	10
1	161.45	199.50	215.71	224.58	230.16	233.99	236.77	238.88	240.54	241.88
2	18.51	19.00	19.16	19.25	19.30	19.33	19.35	19.37	19.39	19.40
3	10.13	9.55	9.28	9.12	9.01	8.94	8.89	8.85	8.81	8.79
4	7.71	6.94	6.59	6.39	6.26	6.16	6.09	6.04	6.00	5.96
5	6.61	5.79	5.41	5.19	5.05	4.95	4.88	4.82	4.77	4.74
6	5.99	5.14	4.76	4.53	4.39	4.28	4.21	4.15	4.10	4.06
7	5.59	4.74	4.35	4.12	3.97	3.87	3.79	3.73	3.68	3.64
8	5.32	4.46	4.07	3.84	3.69	3.58	3.50	3.44	3.39	3.35
9	5.12	4.26	3.86	3.63	3.48	3.37	3.29	3.23	3.18	3.14
10	4.97	4.10	3.71	3.48	3.33	3.22	3.14	3.07	3.02	2.98
11	4.84	3.98	3.59	3.36	3.20	3.10	3.01	2.95	2.90	2.85
12	4.75	3.89	3.49	3.26	3.11	3.00	2.91	2.85	2.80	2.75
13	4.67	3.81	3.41	3.18	3.03	2.92	2.83	2.77	2.71	2.67
14	4.60	3.74	3.34	3.11	2.96	2.85	2.76	2.70	2.65	2.60
15	4.54	3.68	3.29	3.06	2.90	2.79	2.71	2.64	2.59	2.54
16	4.49	3.63	3.24	3.01	2.85	2.74	2.66	2.59	2.54	2.49
17	4.45	3.59	3.20	2.97	2.81	2.70	2.61	2.55	2.49	2.45
18	4.41	3.56	3.16	2.93	2.77	2.66	2.58	2.51	2.46	2.41
19	4.38	3.52	3.13	2.90	2.74	2.63	2.54	2.48	2.42	2.38
20	4.35	3.49	3.10	2.87	2.71	2.60	2.51	2.45	2.39	2.35
21	4.33	3.47	3.07	2.84	2.69	2.57	2.49	2.42	2.37	2.32
22	4.30	3.44	3.05	2.82	2.66	2.55	2.46	2.40	2.34	2.30
23	4.28	3.42	3.03	2.80	2.64	2.53	2.44	2.38	2.32	2.28
24	4.26	3.40	3.01	2.78	2.62	2.51	2.42	2.36	2.30	2.26
25	4.24	3.39	2.99	2.76	2.60	2.49	2.41	2.34	2.28	2.24
26	4.23	3.37	2.98	2.74	2.59	2.47	2.39	2.32	2.27	2.22
27	4.21	3.35	2.96	2.73	2.57	2.46	2.37	2.31	2.25	2.20
28	4.20	3.34	2.95	2.71	2.56	2.45	2.36	2.29	2.24	2.19
29	4.18	3.33	2.93	2.70	2.55	2.43	2.35	2.28	2.22	2.18
30	4.17	3.32	2.92	2.69	2.53	2.42	2.33	2.27	2.21	2.17
31	4.16	3.31	2.91	2.68	2.52	2.41	2.32	2.26	2.20	2.15
32	4.15	3.30	2.90	2.67	2.51	2.40	2.31	2.24	2.19	2.14
33	4.14	3.29	2.89	2.66	2.50	2.39	2.30	2.24	2.18	2.13
34	4.13	3.28	2.88	2.65	2.49	2.38	2.29	2.23	2.17	2.12
35	4.12	3.27	2.87	2.64	2.49	2.37	2.29	2.22	2.16	2.11

Contd...

References

5.1 Critical Value of F *(Contd...)*

36	4.11	3.26	2.87	2.63	2.48	2.36	2.28	2.21	2.15	2.11
37	4.11	3.25	2.86	2.63	2.47	2.36	2.27	2.20	2.15	2.10
38	4.10	3.25	2.85	2.62	2.46	2.35	2.26	2.19	2.14	2.09
39	4.09	3.24	2.85	2.61	2.46	2.34	2.26	2.19	2.13	2.08
40	4.09	3.23	2.84	2.61	2.45	2.34	2.25	2.18	2.12	2.08
41	4.08	3.23	2.83	2.60	2.44	2.33	2.24	2.17	2.12	2.07
42	4.07	3.22	2.83	2.59	2.44	2.32	2.24	2.17	2.11	2.07
43	4.07	3.21	2.82	2.59	2.43	2.32	2.23	2.16	2.11	2.06
44	4.06	3.21	2.82	2.58	2.43	2.31	2.23	2.16	2.10	2.05
45	4.06	3.20	2.81	2.58	2.42	2.31	2.22	2.15	2.10	2.05
46	4.05	3.20	2.81	2.57	2.42	2.30	2.22	2.15	2.09	2.04
47	4.05	3.20	2.80	2.57	2.41	2.30	2.21	2.14	2.09	2.04
48	4.04	3.19	2.80	2.57	2.41	2.30	2.21	2.14	2.08	2.04
49	4.04	3.19	2.79	2.56	2.40	2.29	2.20	2.13	2.08	2.03
50	4.03	3.18	2.79	2.56	2.40	2.29	2.20	2.13	2.07	2.03
51	4.03	3.18	2.79	2.55	2.40	2.28	2.20	2.13	2.07	2.02
52	4.03	3.18	2.78	2.55	2.39	2.28	2.19	2.12	2.07	2.02
53	4.02	3.17	2.78	2.55	2.39	2.28	2.19	2.12	2.06	2.02
54	4.02	3.17	2.78	2.54	2.39	2.27	2.19	2.12	2.06	2.01
55	4.02	3.17	2.77	2.54	2.38	2.27	2.18	2.11	2.06	2.01
56	4.01	3.16	2.77	2.54	2.38	2.27	2.18	2.11	2.05	2.01
57	4.01	3.16	2.77	2.53	2.38	2.26	2.18	2.11	2.05	2.00
58	4.01	3.16	2.76	2.53	2.37	2.26	2.17	2.10	2.05	2.00
59	4.00	3.15	2.76	2.53	2.37	2.26	2.17	2.10	2.04	2.00
60	4.00	3.15	2.76	2.53	2.37	2.25	2.17	2.10	2.04	1.99
61	4.00	3.15	2.76	2.52	2.37	2.25	2.16	2.09	2.04	1.99
62	4.00	3.15	2.75	2.52	2.36	2.25	2.16	2.09	2.04	1.99
63	3.99	3.14	2.75	2.52	2.36	2.25	2.16	2.09	2.03	1.99
64	3.99	3.14	2.75	2.52	2.36	2.24	2.16	2.09	2.03	1.98
65	3.99	3.14	2.75	2.51	2.36	2.24	2.15	2.08	2.03	1.98
66	3.99	3.14	2.74	2.51	2.35	2.24	2.15	2.08	2.03	1.98
67	3.98	3.13	2.74	2.51	2.35	2.24	2.15	2.08	2.02	1.98
68	3.98	3.13	2.74	2.51	2.35	2.24	2.15	2.08	2.02	1.97
69	3.98	3.13	2.74	2.51	2.35	2.23	2.15	2.08	2.02	1.97
70	3.98	3.13	2.74	2.50	2.35	2.23	2.14	2.07	2.02	1.97
71	3.98	3.13	2.73	2.50	2.34	2.23	2.14	2.07	2.02	1.97
72	3.97	3.12	2.73	2.50	2.34	2.23	2.14	2.07	2.01	1.97
73	3.97	3.12	2.73	2.50	2.34	2.23	2.14	2.07	2.01	1.96
74	3.97	3.12	2.73	2.50	2.34	2.22	2.14	2.07	2.01	1.96
75	3.97	3.12	2.73	2.49	2.34	2.22	2.13	2.06	2.01	1.96
76	3.97	3.12	2.73	2.49	2.34	2.22	2.13	2.06	2.01	1.96
77	3.97	3.12	2.72	2.49	2.33	2.22	2.13	2.06	2.00	1.96
78	3.96	3.11	2.72	2.49	2.33	2.22	2.13	2.06	2.00	1.95
79	3.96	3.11	2.72	2.49	2.33	2.22	2.13	2.06	2.00	1.95
80	3.96	3.11	2.72	2.49	2.33	2.21	2.13	2.06	2.00	1.95
81	3.96	3.11	2.72	2.48	2.33	2.21	2.13	2.06	2.00	1.95
82	3.96	3.11	2.72	2.48	2.33	2.21	2.12	2.05	2.00	1.95
83	3.96	3.11	2.72	2.48	2.32	2.21	2.12	2.05	2.00	1.95
84	3.96	3.11	2.71	2.48	2.32	2.21	2.12	2.05	1.99	1.95
85	3.95	3.10	2.71	2.48	2.32	2.21	2.12	2.05	1.99	1.94

Contd...

5.1 Critical Value of F *(Contd...)*

86	3.95	3.10	2.71	2.48	2.32	2.21	2.12	2.05	1.99	1.94
87	3.95	3.10	2.71	2.48	2.32	2.21	2.12	2.05	1.99	1.94
88	3.95	3.10	2.71	2.48	2.32	2.20	2.12	2.05	1.99	1.94
89	3.95	3.10	2.71	2.47	2.32	2.20	2.11	2.04	1.99	1.94
90	3.95	3.10	2.71	2.47	2.32	2.20	2.11	2.04	1.99	1.94
91	3.95	3.10	2.71	2.47	2.32	2.20	2.11	2.04	1.98	1.94
92	3.95	3.10	2.70	2.47	2.31	2.20	2.11	2.04	1.98	1.94
93	3.94	3.09	2.70	2.47	2.31	2.20	2.11	2.04	1.98	1.93
94	3.94	3.09	2.70	2.47	2.31	2.20	2.11	2.04	1.98	1.93
95	3.94	3.09	2.70	2.47	2.31	2.20	2.11	2.04	1.98	1.93
96	3.94	3.09	2.70	2.47	2.31	2.20	2.11	2.04	1.98	1.93
97	3.94	3.09	2.70	2.47	2.31	2.19	2.11	2.04	1.98	1.93
98	3.94	3.09	2.70	2.47	2.31	2.19	2.10	2.03	1.98	1.93
99	3.94	3.09	2.70	2.46	2.31	2.19	2.10	2.03	1.98	1.93
100	3.94	3.09	2.70	2.46	2.31	2.19	2.10	2.03	1.98	1.93

Critical values of F for the 0.01 significance level:

	1	2	3	4	5	6	7	8	9	10
1	4052.19	4999.52	5403.34	5624.62	5763.65	5858.97	5928.33	5981.10	6022.50	6055.85
2	98.50	99.00	99.17	99.25	99.30	99.33	99.36	99.37	99.39	99.40
3	34.12	30.82	29.46	28.71	28.24	27.91	27.67	27.49	27.35	27.23
4	21.20	18.00	16.69	15.98	15.52	15.21	14.98	14.80	14.66	14.55
5	16.26	13.27	12.06	11.39	10.97	10.67	10.46	10.29	10.16	10.05
6	13.75	10.93	9.78	9.15	8.75	8.47	8.26	8.10	7.98	7.87
7	12.25	9.55	8.45	7.85	7.46	7.19	6.99	6.84	6.72	6.62
8	11.26	8.65	7.59	7.01	6.63	6.37	6.18	6.03	5.91	5.81
9	10.56	8.02	6.99	6.42	6.06	5.80	5.61	5.47	5.35	5.26
10	10.04	7.56	6.55	5.99	5.64	5.39	5.20	5.06	4.94	4.85
11	9.65	7.21	6.22	5.67	5.32	5.07	4.89	4.74	4.63	4.54
12	9.33	6.93	5.95	5.41	5.06	4.82	4.64	4.50	4.39	4.30
13	9.07	6.70	5.74	5.21	4.86	4.62	4.44	4.30	4.19	4.10
14	8.86	6.52	5.56	5.04	4.70	4.46	4.28	4.14	4.03	3.94
15	8.68	6.36	5.42	4.89	4.56	4.32	4.14	4.00	3.90	3.81
16	8.53	6.23	5.29	4.77	4.44	4.20	4.03	3.89	3.78	3.69
17	8.40	6.11	5.19	4.67	4.34	4.10	3.93	3.79	3.68	3.59
18	8.29	6.01	5.09	4.58	4.25	4.02	3.84	3.71	3.60	3.51
19	8.19	5.93	5.01	4.50	4.17	3.94	3.77	3.63	3.52	3.43
20	8.10	5.85	4.94	4.43	4.10	3.87	3.70	3.56	3.46	3.37
21	8.02	5.78	4.87	4.37	4.04	3.81	3.64	3.51	3.40	3.31
22	7.95	5.72	4.82	4.31	3.99	3.76	3.59	3.45	3.35	3.26
23	7.88	5.66	4.77	4.26	3.94	3.71	3.54	3.41	3.30	3.21
24	7.82	5.61	4.72	4.22	3.90	3.67	3.50	3.36	3.26	3.17
25	7.77	5.57	4.68	4.18	3.86	3.63	3.46	3.32	3.22	3.13
26	7.72	5.53	4.64	4.14	3.82	3.59	3.42	3.29	3.18	3.09
27	7.68	5.49	4.60	4.11	3.79	3.56	3.39	3.26	3.15	3.06
28	7.64	5.45	4.57	4.07	3.75	3.53	3.36	3.23	3.12	3.03
29	7.60	5.42	4.54	4.05	3.73	3.50	3.33	3.20	3.09	3.01
30	7.56	5.39	4.51	4.02	3.70	3.47	3.31	3.17	3.07	2.98
31	7.53	5.36	4.48	3.99	3.68	3.45	3.28	3.15	3.04	2.96
32	7.50	5.34	4.46	3.97	3.65	3.43	3.26	3.13	3.02	2.93

Contd...

References

5.1 Critical Value of F *(Contd...)*

33	7.47	5.31	4.44	3.95	3.63	3.41	3.24	3.11	3.00	2.91
34	7.44	5.29	4.42	3.93	3.61	3.39	3.22	3.09	2.98	2.89
35	7.42	5.27	4.40	3.91	3.59	3.37	3.20	3.07	2.96	2.88
36	7.40	5.25	4.38	3.89	3.57	3.35	3.18	3.05	2.95	2.86
37	7.37	5.23	4.36	3.87	3.56	3.33	3.17	3.04	2.93	2.84
38	7.35	5.21	4.34	3.86	3.54	3.32	3.15	3.02	2.92	2.83
39	7.33	5.19	4.33	3.84	3.53	3.31	3.14	3.01	2.90	2.81
40	7.31	5.18	4.31	3.83	3.51	3.29	3.12	2.99	2.89	2.80
41	7.30	5.16	4.30	3.82	3.50	3.28	3.11	2.98	2.88	2.79
42	7.28	5.15	4.29	3.80	3.49	3.27	3.10	2.97	2.86	2.78
43	7.26	5.14	4.27	3.79	3.48	3.25	3.09	2.96	2.85	2.76
44	7.25	5.12	4.26	3.78	3.47	3.24	3.08	2.95	2.84	2.75
45	7.23	5.11	4.25	3.77	3.45	3.23	3.07	2.94	2.83	2.74
46	7.22	5.10	4.24	3.76	3.44	3.22	3.06	2.93	2.82	2.73
47	7.21	5.09	4.23	3.75	3.43	3.21	3.05	2.92	2.81	2.72
48	7.19	5.08	4.22	3.74	3.43	3.20	3.04	2.91	2.80	2.72
49	7.18	5.07	4.21	3.73	3.42	3.20	3.03	2.90	2.79	2.71
50	7.17	5.06	4.20	3.72	3.41	3.19	3.02	2.89	2.79	2.70
51	7.16	5.05	4.19	3.71	3.40	3.18	3.01	2.88	2.78	2.69
52	7.15	5.04	4.18	3.70	3.39	3.17	3.01	2.87	2.77	2.68
53	7.14	5.03	4.17	3.70	3.38	3.16	3.00	2.87	2.76	2.68
54	7.13	5.02	4.17	3.69	3.38	3.16	2.99	2.86	2.76	2.67
55	7.12	5.01	4.16	3.68	3.37	3.15	2.98	2.85	2.75	2.66
56	7.11	5.01	4.15	3.67	3.36	3.14	2.98	2.85	2.74	2.66
57	7.10	5.00	4.15	3.67	3.36	3.14	2.97	2.84	2.74	2.65
58	7.09	4.99	4.14	3.66	3.35	3.13	2.97	2.84	2.73	2.64
59	7.09	4.98	4.13	3.66	3.35	3.12	2.96	2.83	2.72	2.64
60	7.08	4.98	4.13	3.65	3.34	3.12	2.95	2.82	2.72	2.63
61	7.07	4.97	4.12	3.64	3.33	3.11	2.95	2.82	2.71	2.63
62	7.06	4.97	4.11	3.64	3.33	3.11	2.94	2.81	2.71	2.62
63	7.06	4.96	4.11	3.63	3.32	3.10	2.94	2.81	2.70	2.62
64	7.05	4.95	4.10	3.63	3.32	3.10	2.93	2.80	2.70	2.61
65	7.04	4.95	4.10	3.62	3.31	3.09	2.93	2.80	2.69	2.61
66	7.04	4.94	4.09	3.62	3.31	3.09	2.92	2.79	2.69	2.60
67	7.03	4.94	4.09	3.61	3.30	3.08	2.92	2.79	2.68	2.60
68	7.02	4.93	4.08	3.61	3.30	3.08	2.91	2.79	2.68	2.59
69	7.02	4.93	4.08	3.60	3.30	3.08	2.91	2.78	2.68	2.59
70	7.01	4.92	4.07	3.60	3.29	3.07	2.91	2.78	2.67	2.59
71	7.01	4.92	4.07	3.60	3.29	3.07	2.90	2.77	2.67	2.58
72	7.00	4.91	4.07	3.59	3.28	3.06	2.90	2.77	2.66	2.58
73	7.00	4.91	4.06	3.59	3.28	3.06	2.90	2.77	2.66	2.57
74	6.99	4.90	4.06	3.58	3.28	3.06	2.89	2.76	2.66	2.57
75	6.99	4.90	4.05	3.58	3.27	3.05	2.89	2.76	2.65	2.57
76	6.98	4.90	4.05	3.58	3.27	3.05	2.88	2.76	2.65	2.56
77	6.98	4.89	4.05	3.57	3.27	3.05	2.88	2.75	2.65	2.56
78	6.97	4.89	4.04	3.57	3.26	3.04	2.88	2.75	2.64	2.56
79	6.97	4.88	4.04	3.57	3.26	3.04	2.87	2.75	2.64	2.55
80	6.96	4.88	4.04	3.56	3.26	3.04	2.87	2.74	2.64	2.55
81	6.96	4.88	4.03	3.56	3.25	3.03	2.87	2.74	2.63	2.55
82	6.95	4.87	4.03	3.56	3.25	3.03	2.87	2.74	2.63	2.55

Contd...

5.1 Critical Value of F *(Contd...)*

83	6.95	4.87	4.03	3.55	3.25	3.03	2.86	2.73	2.63	2.54
84	6.95	4.87	4.02	3.55	3.24	3.03	2.86	2.73	2.63	2.54
85	6.94	4.86	4.02	3.55	3.24	3.02	2.86	2.73	2.62	2.54
86	6.94	4.86	4.02	3.55	3.24	3.02	2.85	2.73	2.62	2.53
87	6.94	4.86	4.02	3.54	3.24	3.02	2.85	2.72	2.62	2.53
88	6.93	4.86	4.01	3.54	3.23	3.01	2.85	2.72	2.62	2.53
89	6.93	4.85	4.01	3.54	3.23	3.01	2.85	2.72	2.61	2.53
90	6.93	4.85	4.01	3.54	3.23	3.01	2.85	2.72	2.61	2.52
91	6.92	4.85	4.00	3.53	3.23	3.01	2.84	2.71	2.61	2.52
92	6.92	4.84	4.00	3.53	3.22	3.00	2.84	2.71	2.61	2.52
93	6.92	4.84	4.00	3.53	3.22	3.00	2.84	2.71	2.60	2.52
94	6.91	4.84	4.00	3.53	3.22	3.00	2.84	2.71	2.60	2.52
95	6.91	4.84	4.00	3.52	3.22	3.00	2.83	2.70	2.60	2.51
96	6.91	4.83	3.99	3.52	3.21	3.00	2.83	2.70	2.60	2.51
97	6.90	4.83	3.99	3.52	3.21	2.99	2.83	2.70	2.60	2.51
98	6.90	4.83	3.99	3.52	3.21	2.99	2.83	2.70	2.59	2.51
99	6.90	4.83	3.99	3.52	3.21	2.99	2.83	2.70	2.59	2.51
100	6.90	4.82	3.98	3.51	3.21	2.99	2.82	2.69	2.59	2.50

Index

A

Academic Writing 121

Academic Writing 127

Annual Reports 17

ANOVA 78

Applications 5

Applications of Business Research 5

Assumptions 105

B

Bivariate Analysis 78

Business 2

Business Organization 2

Business Research 2, 3

C

Causal Research 21

Chi-Square Test 98

Cluster Sampling 52

Collecting Primary Data 32

Company Newsletters and Reports 27

Comparison of Self-Administered, 35

Concept of Measurement 39

Concept of Scaling 40

Constant Sum 43

Content Validity 48

Convenience Sampling 52

Convergent Validity 48

Correlation 104

Correlation and Regression Analysis 104

Correlation 105

Correlational 23

Creswell 2

Criteria for Evaluating Secondary Sources 26

Criterion Validity 48

Cronbach Alpha 55

Cronbach Alpha Test for Reliability 55

D

Data analysis 66

Data Visualization 68

Decision 4

Decision Making 3

Degree of Freedom 100

Dependent 110

Descriptive Analysis 70

Descriptive Research 21

Descriptive 22

Determination of Sample Size 53

Direct 34

Discriminant Analysis 117

Discriminant Validity 48

Disproportional Sampling 53

Dissertation 10

(149)

150 A Concise Handbook of Business Research

Dissertation Reports 17

Dissertation/Project Work 10

Doing One-Way ANOVA 84

E

Emails Techniques 35

Estimating Pearson's Correlation Coefficient 106

Ethical Issues 12

Ethics 12

Excel 57, 70

Expected Frequencies 100

Exploratory Factor Analysis (EFA) 115

Exploratory Research 21

External Validity 24

F

Face Validity 48

Factor Analysis 115

Factor Analysis 115

Fake Data 13

Form & Design 44

Formulation 13

Free Software Grammarly 127

Fundamentals of Scale Evaluation 47

G

Generalizability 49

Government Reports 27

I

Important Terms Associated 109

Independent Variables 110

Indirect Observation 34

Internal 24

Interval Scale 41

Interview 32

Interview Method 33

In-text Citation 121, 122

Introduction to R 58

Itemized Ratings 43

J

Journal Articles 27

Judgment (Purposive) Sampling 52

L

Likert Scale 43

Linear Regression Analysis 109

Literature Review 17

M

Magazines 17, 27

Mail 35

Making 4

Management Decision Problem Research Problem 6

Managerial 4

Manipulate Data 13

Marketing 17

Measurement 4, 39

Method 32

Method of Analysis 66

Methods 19, 52

Mode of Presenting A Questionnaire 45

Index 151

MS -Word 2016 122
MS-Excel 51
Multivariate Analysis 115

N

Nature of Business Research 4
Newsletters 17
Newspapers 16, 27
Nominal Scale 40
Nonparticipant Observation 34
Non-Probability 52
Non-Probability Sampling 51
Null and Alternate Hypothesis 82

O

Objective 16, 32
Observation Method 33
Observations 35
Observed Frequencies 100
OLS Regression 109
One-Way ANOVA 84
Open Source Journal 17
Ordinal Scale 40

P

Paired Comparison 42
Participant 34
Participants 12
Pearson's Correlation 105
Performance Appraisal 17
Permission 13
Plagiarism 125
Plagiarism Detection 126

Presentation 5
Primary Data 31
Primary Data 31
Principal Component Analysis (PCA) 115
Privacy 12
Probability Sampling 51
Problem 16
Procedures 19
Project Report 10, 17
Proportional 53
Purpose Statement in Your Project/ Thesis. 15

Q

Qualitative Research 22
Questionnaire 32, 44
Questionnaire Method 32
Questionnaire-Form & Design 44
Quota Sampling 53

R

Random Sample 34
Random Sample Collection Method 34
Rank Order 42
Ranking Scales 42
Rating Scale 41, 42
References 122
Referencing 121
Referencing and In-text Citation 121
Regression Analysis 104, 111

152 A Concise Handbook of Business Research

Regression Model 109
Reliability 47
Research 2
Research Design 19
Research Problem 13
Research Process 6
Research Proposal 9
Rough Estimate 55
Studio 59

S

Sample 50
Sample Size 55
Sample Table 53
Sampling 39, 49
Sampling Techniques 50
Scale Evaluation 47
Scales of Measurement 40
Scaling 39
Scaling Techniques 42
Secondary Data Research 25
Secondary Data Sources 26
Secondary Data 26
Self-Administered 35
Semantic Differential 43
Shodhganga 15, 17

Significance Level 83
Simple Random Sampling 51
Snowball Sampling 52
Statistical Data 57
Statistical Data Analysis 57
Statistical Test 82
Stratified Sampling 51
Style 19
Supervisor 20
Survey 32, 35
Survey Methods 32
Survey vs Observations 35
Syndicate Research 28
Synopsis 9
Systematic 4
Systematic Sampling 51

T

Teachers 17
Telephone 35

U

Unit of Analysis 21

V

Validation 5
Validity 48
Validity in Experiment 24

❏❏❏